CONFERENCE PROCEEDINGS

RAND

The Global Course of the Information Revolution: Political, Economic, and Social Consequences

Proceedings of an International Conference

Richard O. Hundley, Robert H. Anderson, Tora K. Bikson, James A. Dewar, Jerrold Green, Martin Libicki, and C. Richard Neu

National Defense Research Institute

Preface

The National Intelligence Council (NIC) is undertaking a systematic research and development program on broad, crosscutting issues for the next millennium; this constitutes the DCI's Strategic Estimates Program. One of these strategic estimates focuses on developing a better understanding of the future course of the information revolution throughout the world over the next 10-20 years.

The NIC has asked RAND to take the lead in this effort to chart the future course of the information revolution. As the first major step in a multi-year program of research, RAND convened a major international conference in Washington DC in November 1999, focusing on the political/governmental, business/financial, and social/cultural dimensions of the information revolution, as they are unfolding in different areas of the world.

This report presents the proceedings of that conference.

This research is sponsored by the National Intelligence Council, and monitored by the National Intelligence Officer (NIO) for Science and Technology. It is being conducted by the Acquisition and Technology Policy Center of RAND's National Defense Research Institute (NDRI). NDRI is a federally funded research and development center sponsored by the Office of the Secretary of defense, the Joint Staff, the defense agencies, and the unified commands.

Contents

Part IV. CONCLUDING REMARKS

APPENDICIES

Figures

Tables

Summary

The information revolution is bringing about profound changes in many aspects of life. RAND has embarked on a three-year effort, sponsored by the National Intelligence Council, to chart the future course of these changes over the next 10-20 years, all over the world. As a first step in this effort, RAND convened a conference on political/governmental, business/financial, and social/cultural trends driven by the information revolution, as they manifest themselves in various nations and regions. This conference was held in Washington, DC on November 16-18, 1999, with participants from North America, Europe, and the Asian Pacific region, covering a broad cross section of intellectual disciplines.

The Political/Governmental Dimension of the Information Revolution

Regarding the political/governmental arena, conference discussions focused primarily on possible changes in the role of the nation state as a result of the information revolution. Such changes were seen as occurring for two general reasons:

- Traditional mechanisms of governance (e.g., taxation, regulation and licensing, etc.) are becoming increasingly problematic, as the information revolution allows action beyond the reach of national governments.

- The distribution of political power is changing, as new non-state actors are being empowered by the information revolution, in the business, social, and political realms, at the sub-national, trans-national, and supra-national levels.

Governments will have to find mechanisms to deal with these changes and with these new actors. Different nations may take different approaches. How they do this will affect the future course of the information revolution in their regions and go to define the role(s) of the nation state in the information age.

We elaborate on this theme in Section 4.

The Business/Financial Dimension of the Information Revolution

Conference discussions focused on two aspects of IT-driven changes in the business and financial world: the rise of electronic commerce, and new models for the internal organization and functioning of business enterprises and for their external interactions with customers, suppliers, and competitors.

E-commerce is growing rapidly, in both the business-to-business and business-to-consumer segments. It demolishes many existing barriers to market entry. Stage one of e-commerce adoption usually focuses on cost reduction via increased efficiencies and effectiveness within existing business models. This often tends to attract companies "offshore," to suppliers in other countries with lower labor costs (yet a high standard of education), good (local) infrastructures with global connectivity, and tax breaks for exports. Stage two of e-commerce adoption involves revolutionary change in the business model. This requires skills in innovation and business change that are likely to be incompatible with foreign out-sourcing. Such skills are more likely to be found in "clusters": geographic concentrations of interconnected companies and institutions in a particular field.

Besides its impact on business, e-commerce is also affecting governments and people in fundamental ways. It affects *government* by increasing efficiency and changing interactions with the outside world, affecting the speed and availability of information, and challenging existing regulatory frameworks. It affects *people* by reducing prices, creating new products and services and increasing choice, changing working methods, and, on the negative side, by creating possibilities of social exclusion.

In parallel with the spread of e-commerce, new business models are emerging. These models are characterized by:

- The centrality of the customer, the dominant factor in business today, and of competition, fundamental to the development and progress of a business enterprise.

- A non-linear world defining business processes, in which businesses are driven by information from the real world, not the internal company world, and must operate in real time.

- A customer services approach to developing everything, with technology and business closely integrated.

- Globalization, in all its manifestations.

- A redefinition of basic business functions, with new paradigms for product, service, delivery, support, and pricing.

These changes look profound and disturbing to some (in the business world and elsewhere), but the business community and the broader society are beginning to adapt. The course of this adaptation will vary from nation to nation, and will be affected, among other things, by the structure of the capital markets in different countries: the availability of funding for new IT-related businesses and concepts and the manner of the funding process (i.e., the vagaries of getting funding, listings, capital, acquisitions, etc.) directly impact the growth and development of new IT industries in any given region.

We elaborate on these themes in Section 5.

The Social/Cultural Dimension of the Information Revolution

Regarding the social/cultural implications of the information revolution, conference discussions focused on the developing world, not the developed (i.e., OECD) world, and highlighted contrasting views. One view hypothesized that the information revolution is likely to bring with it significant change and unrest within developing areas of the world. In particular, it was argued that in those developing areas, technology tends to exacerbate differences within a society, with a technologically savvy, highly educated, and IT conversant elite juxtaposed with a technologically unsophisticated, undereducated group of people who largely have been passed over by the information revolution.

In this view, globalization of information exacerbates societal cleavages and is likely to destabilize some governments in the developing world. Further, it aids trans-national movements, creates new sources of authority, and widens socio-political gaps. If current trends persist, we can expect to see more political movements using IT as an element of political dissent, a growing hostility toward political elites in a number of settings, and increasing alienation in a number of sectors -- in the developing world.

A second view, widely held at the conference, was that things are not that bad. The picture painted by the first view may hold in some areas of the Middle East and South America, but is not generally applicable in much of the rest of the developing world.

Proponents of both of these views agreed that generalizations about the cultural and social dimensions of the information revolution are exceedingly difficult to formulate. While there are certain universalities which can be identified, there are also regional and national peculiarities which are not always that easy to ascertain.

We elaborate on these themes in Section 6.

A Vision of the Information Revolution Future: "The Great Information Revolution Attractor"

Across the many, highly varied conference discussions, a shared picture emerges of the world towards which the information revolution is driving humanity. This future world should be thought of as a destination towards which all regions and nations are being drawn, at varying rates and from varying distances removed. By analogy with the "Great Attractor" in astronomy (a region 200 million light-years away towards which all of the galaxies in the vicinity of the Milky Way are being drawn), we term this future world the "great information revolution attractor." It is characterized by a number of interrelated features, including:

- *A rise in "information work" and "information workers,"* as an ever increasing fraction of economic activity and the overall workforce, with a broad range of consequences.

- *New business models,* for the internal organization and functioning of business enterprises, and for their external interactions with customers, suppliers, and competitors.

- *The rise of electronic commerce,* as a major form of economic activity, with accompanying changes in the nature and structure of markets and the elimination of a wide variety of "middlemen" heretofore facilitating economic transitions.

- *Challenges to the power and authority of the nation state,* for a variety of reasons (including the two immediately following).

- *The creation of a wide variety of sub-national, trans-national and supra-national groupings, communities, organizations and enterprises,* in the business, social, and political realms, often largely beyond the control of individual nation states.

- *An ever increasing porosity of national borders,* to trade and financial flows, to population flows, and to the flow of ideas, entertainment, and culture.

- *Many new winners, and also many new losers.* Some individuals, groups, localities, nations and regions will gain (in power, influence and material well being) as a result of the information revolution; others will lose. All will not share equally in the benefits.

- *New fault lines, within and between nations.* The widening gulfs between the educated, wealthy, and cyber-privileged of all nations, on the one hand, and the not-so-lucky of all nations on the other, will lead to fault lines within nations as well as between nations.

Differences in Regional Emphasis Regarding the Information Revolution Future

Different regions of the world react differently to this presumed future, to this "great IR attractor": some accept it more or less unquestioningly; some wish to modify it; some strive to achieve it; some try to resist it. As reflected in the breakout group discussions during the conference, these differing emphases appear to be as follows:

North America

The predominant North American attitude could be characterized as "information revolution determinism." The information revolution is viewed as being inevitable. It will run its course no matter what. Backlashes of various forms are expected to occur, but these are not considered likely to sufficiently retard or modify the process.

Concerns are expressed regarding the disenfranchisement of the "information poor," leading to increased social stress and stratification. Conflicts over privacy are also expected.

But in the end, the information revolution is expected to prevail. North America is in the camp that accepts the information revolution as being more or less irresistible and socially beneficial.

We elaborate on this North American view in Section 8.

Europe

In Europe there is much more of a focus on realizing (economic) value from the information revolution <u>while</u> at the same time maintaining and protecting existing cultural and social values. Europeans believe that they can and must actively shape the course of the information revolution to achieve these ends.

There is much more of a determination to alleviate disparities (between winners and losers) insofar as possible, than appears to be the case in the U.S. (Canada may be closer to Europe than to the U.S. on this issue.) There are also major concerns about maintaining privacy. (Currently, these concerns regarding privacy are greater in Europe than in the U.S.)

Europe is in the camp that wants to shape the course of the information revolution, to suit its own ends. To what extent it can do this remains to be seen.

We elaborate on this European view in Section 9.

Asia Pacific Region

The emphasis in the Asia Pacific region is on realizing value from the information revolution -- primarily economic value. There is less concern with disparities, and less concern about privacy (possibly because of the "communal" nature of Asian culture). The prevailing attitude appears to be: "Don't worry about losers; concentrate on becoming a winner." There appears to be widespread confidence that many/most Asian countries can become winners.

The Asia Pacific region appears to be in the camp that is striving to achieve the information revolution, and is generally confident that it can do so.

We elaborate on this Asian Pacific view in Section 10.

Middle East, Africa, and South Asia

This part of the world is often characterized by strong differences in focus between leadership/elite groups and mass citizenry. Many leaders/elites want, and use, the benefits of information technology -- but are wary of its influences on the citizenry.

In some major nations (e.g., India), there is a determination not to be left behind by the information revolution (i.e., to be one of the winners, not one of the losers). As one conference participant from this part of the world said: "We missed out on the industrial revolution; we don't want to miss out on the information revolution." In these nations, there is much discussion of what it takes to get access to and successfully exploit information technology, to raise the nation/region (economically, socially, etc.) But it often proves difficult to expand "islands" of information-revolution expertise, both within nations and to the rest of the countries in the region.

Some other nations' leaders/elites in the region may already anticipate losing, and may be starting to imagine dire consequences. But many citizens are unaffected and unconcerned now, and will be into the indefinite future.

Especially in this region, much of the information revolution emphasis may be on non-Internet technologies: e.g., wireless telephony, accessible satellite TV broadcasts, photo copier and fax machines, audio and video cassettes, etc.

Many in the Middle East, Africa, and South Asia want to use the information revolution to better themselves and their countries, but with widely varying abilities to do so.

We elaborate on this Middle Eastern, African, and South Asian view in Section 11.

Some Inferred Candidate National Models of the Information Revolution Future

The conference discussions did not explicitly develop a comprehensive set of models of what the information revolution future might be like in various nations and regions throughout the world. However, from those discussions it is possible to infer the following candidate set of national models of the information revolution future:

- *IR Achievers.* These are nations that have substantially attained most/all of the characteristics of "the great IR attractor." Information work and information workers represent an ever increasing fraction of the economy and the workforce; new, information-based business models and electronic commerce are spreading throughout the business and financial communities; many/most segments of society are well into the information age, and substantially "wired" into the global arena. Australia is one example (among several) of a nation that is today an IR Achiever. (This country assignment, as well as the others that follow, is very preliminary and meant merely to be illustrative.)

- *IR Drivers.* These are nations that go well beyond being merely an IR Achiever. They not only have attained most/all of the (then) existing characteristics of "the great IR attractor," but go well beyond this to create new characteristics, new manifestations of the information revolution. The U.S. is the best, but not the only, example of an IR Driver nation today.

- *IR Strivers.* These are nations that are working very hard to reach" the great IR attractor," but still have a considerable way to go, with the final result still in some doubt. Taiwan is an example of a nation that today is an IR Striver.

- *IR Modifiers.* These are nations that are not satisfied with one or more characteristics of "the great IR attractor" towards which they are being drawn, and wish to actively shape and modify those characteristics to suit their own ends. They are trying to change the course of the information revolution, insofar as it applies to them. Singapore is a clear example today of an IR Modifier. It is trying to realize all of the benefits of the information revolution in the economic sphere, while at the same time strictly controlling developments in the social/cultural sphere.

- *IR Veneer Societies.* These are nations in which a small fraction of the society is participating in the information revolution and well into the information age, with the vast bulk of the population still in the industrial or even the agricultural age. India is a clear example today of an IR Veneer Society. It has geographical clusters of high technology (e.g., around Bangalore), with software (and other) companies fully participating in the global information economy and some even on the NASDAQ stock exchange. At the same time, the vast majority of Indian citizens (probably 95% or more) are uninvolved in and unaffected by the information revolution.

- *IR Left-Behinds.* These are nations that have been more or less totally left behind by the information revolution. It has passed them by, for whatever reasons (most often socioeconomic). They are not involved, and largely unaware. Zaire is one such example, today, of an IR Left-Behind.

- *IR Luddites.* These are nations that, for whatever reason, actively oppose the course of the information revolution. They want to opt out. They don't want to participate. They don't want it happening in their society. They are more or less totally opposed to the changes being brought on by the information revolution. North Korea may be an example today of an IR Luddite.

- *Sore IR Losers.* These are nations that are unhappy left-behinds. They feel themselves losing out, as the information revolution progresses, and they are not happy with this outcome. It is not clear that any nation fits into this category today. But some could in the future.

This set of future models appears to span the range of situations suggested during the conference discussions. Most nations and regions should fit into one or another of these categories, insofar as the information revolution is concerned. (At any given time, some of these models could be empty sets, and some nations could be in more than one category.) We intend using this set of models as a point of departure during our future efforts to chart the worldwide course of the information revolution. (During these future efforts, this set of models will most likely evolve and change.)

What Comes Next

This November 1999 conference was just a beginning. The next step in our multi-year effort to chart the future course of the information revolution will be a conference in the Spring of 2000 focused on the technology underpinnings of the revolution. This conference will address the question: how may these technology drivers change over the next 10-20 years?

Following that, we expect to carry out a number of in-depth studies and small workshops focused on specific topics identified during the November 1999 conference as requiring further investigation.

Once these are (substantially) complete, we anticipate holding two more major international conferences, preferably in Europe and in Asia, to expose and vet our results before a wider international audience, thereby broadening and deepening our models of the future course of the information revolution throughout the world.

We elaborate on these future efforts in Section 13.

Acknowledgments

The conference on "The Global Course of the Information Revolution: Political, Economic, and Social Consequences" was truly a group effort. The results presented here are due to the collaborative efforts of all of the participants, who are listed in Appendix A. They all deserve a major vote of thanks.

Special thanks are due to the individuals who presented prepared talks at the conference: Dr. Jon Alterman, Dr. Robert Anderson, Professor V. S. Arunachalam, Professor Paul Bracken, Mr. Colin Crook, Dr. James Dewar, Dr. William Drake, Professor Francis Fukuyama, Mr. Hideo Miyashita, Professor M. J. Norton, Mr. Larry Press, and Professor Ernest Wilson.

Special thanks are also due to the individuals who served as moderators of the plenary sessions and leaders of the breakout groups: Dr. Tora Bikson, Mr. David Gompert, Dr. Jerrold Green, Dr. James Mulvenon, Dr. C. Richard Neu, Mr. Ian Pearson, and Professor Ernest Wilson.

The conference chairman would also like to thank the rapporteurs -- Dr. Robert Anderson, Dr. Tora Bikson, Dr. James Dewar, Dr. Jerrold Green, Dr. Martin Libicki, and Dr. C. Richard Neu -- without whose efforts this report could not have been completed.

Finally, thanks are also due to Dr. Lawrence Gershwin, the NIO for S&T, without whose vision and support this conference would not have been possible.

Dr. Richard O. Hundley
Conference Chairman

1. Introduction

Conference Rapporteur: Richard Hundley

RAND is embarked on a three-year effort to chart the likely future course of the information revolution throughout the world over the next 10-20 years, in all its various dimensions.[1] This is intended to be a broad, multi-disciplinary effort, employing a mixture of conferences, workshops, and in-depth studies with a broad range of participants from both inside and outside of RAND, covering all relevant disciplines, to lay out a family of possible "futures" describing the likely course of the information revolution as it plays out in various nations and regions.[2]

The first major step in this effort was a conference on political/governmental, business/financial, and social/cultural trends driven by the information revolution, as they manifest themselves in various nations and regions. This conference was held in Washington, DC on November 16-18, 1999, with participants from North America, Europe, and the Asian Pacific region, covering a broad cross section of intellectual disciplines. This report presents the proceedings of that conference.

The specific aims of this conference were threefold:

- To explore the range of existing views about how the information revolution will influence political, economic, and social conditions and developments throughout the world; how advances in information technology and their applications may create or exacerbate tensions in any of these spheres; and how the consequences of the information revolution in one sphere may be linked to consequences in another.

- To identify some of the factors that may be key in shaping the course and the consequences of the information revolution in different countries.

---

[1] This effort is being carried out in support of the Information Revolution initiative of the National Intelligence Council's Strategic Estimates Program.

[2] We are not trying to predict one "future" for each nation or region around the world, but rather a range of possible futures.

- To lay the groundwork for constructing examples of alternative scenarios of how the information revolution will play out in different countries.

We were most fortunate in the caliber of the participants at this conference: 43 senior-level individuals from government, academia, and the private sector in North America, Europe, and the Asia Pacific region, whose collective breadth of experience and depth of expertise covered most aspects of the information revolution, as it is manifesting itself throughout the world. Among the participants were experts on North America, Europe, the Middle East, Africa, and most of the Asia Pacific region (including China, Japan, the rest of East Asia, South Asia, and Australia). The participants' names and organizational affiliations are given in Appendix A.

The conference began with an initial plenary session devoted to broad organizational and social consequences of the information revolution, and to its technology underpinnings.[3] Sections 2 and 3 of this report summarize the course of this session. Next came a series of plenary sessions devoted to various dimensions of the information revolution, to explore themes recurring throughout the world. The deliberations of these sessions are summarized in Section 4 (the political/governmental dimension), Section 5 (the business/financial dimension), and Section 6 (the social/cultural dimension).

Following the plenary sessions, the conference began its discussion of the different ways in which the information revolution may proceed in various regions of the world by considering three national/regional snapshots: Japan, India, and Africa. These snapshots are presented in Section 7.

The conference participants then divided into a set of four breakout groups, covering different regions of the world, to address how the information revolution may play out in each of their areas. Section 8 (North, Central, and South America), Section 9 (Europe), Section 10 (the Asia Pacific region), and Section 11 (Middle East, Africa, and South Asia) present the results of these breakout group discussions.[4]

As the reader will see from pursuing these various sections, the conference discussions covered a broad range of topics in considerable depth, and generated a rich set of observations regarding the course of the information revolution

----

[3] This session, and all subsequent plenary sessions, began with prepared talks to serve as a point of departure, followed by an extensive audience discussion period to capture the collective perspective of all the participants.

[4] The reader will note that each breakout group took a somewhat different approach. We view this as of positive value.

throughout the world. A number of major themes emerged during these discussions. These are integrated and summarized in Section 12.

As indicated earlier, this conference was merely the beginning of a multi-year effort to chart the future worldwide course of the information revolution. Section 13 describes what we expect will come next.

Appendix B presents the complete conference agenda, including the titles and speakers for all of the prepared talks presented at the conference.

Part I.

Some Initial Considerations

2. Social and Organizational Consequences of the Information Revolution

Speaker: Francis Fukuyama
Rapporteur: C. Richard Neu

The first substantive session of the conference was devoted to a discussion of the social and organizational consequences of the transition into the information age.

The speaker suggested that something we might reasonably call the information revolution has in fact been underway (at least in the industrialized world) for more than thirty years. He noted the declining share of populations in the industrialized world engaged in manufacturing and the rising "information content" of total economic output. As a consequence of this rising information content, the returns to education are increasing, widening the income and social gaps between more- and less-educated workers. As the advantages of education have become increasingly apparent, the overall level of education in most industrial countries has risen to unprecedented levels. The discussion leader noted that these higher levels of education might create new social and political dynamics. And as work has become more mental and less physical, many new opportunities have been created for women.

The information age has allowed and required changes in organizational structures. The rationale for centralized, hierarchical structures--in firms, in governmental agencies, and in other institutions--is passing. When communication was slow, costly, or cumbersome, vertical structures were efficient because they minimized the necessary flow of information and the associated transaction costs. Much cheaper and easier communication is giving rise to flatter structures characterized by much more horizontal communication. Moreover, hierarchies have a way of slowing and distorting information flows. The direct exchange of information through a flat, networked structure that are facilitated by advancing information technology today provides an important efficiency advantage for organizations that can create the right structures.

Flatter organizational structures place a higher value on social networks and on informal communication than did older hierarchical structures. The somewhat ironic result is that advances in information technology have increased the importance of face-to-face communication, and with it the importance of regional concentrations of effort.

Economic and organizational changes can have important social consequences, this speaker noted. He pointed, for example, to the "displacement" of male blue-collar workers from the central positions they occupied in the old, manufacturing-dominated economy. He went on to speculate that the disruption of these traditional economic roles had led to changes in family life--more divorce, less cohesion within the family, etc.

This speaker dismissed claims that the information revolution has weakened social connections in the United States and in other industrialized countries. What has changed, he argued is not the number or the strength of social connections, but their radius. That is, the information revolution has allowed individuals to form social connections with like-minded folk who are not part of the same physically local community. Freed from the restrictions imposed by geography, each of us can now have multiple identities, arising from the different "communities" with which we are able to interact.

The ultimate social consequences of these developments remain to be seen. Will the growing ease of communication lead benignly to improved access to information tailored to individual needs? Or will it create a more fractionated society with few shared cultural values? Perhaps both.

In the political realm, the speaker noted, the information revolution seems to have provided a boost for democracy. It seems also, however, to be leading to more social stratification, although it is not clear that this reflects the rise of information technology per se or the increasing returns to education. (But are the two really different?)

Easier communications have also increased the effectiveness of non-governmental organizations (NGOs). With improved access to information, NGOs are more independent of governments. Sometimes this can cause problems for governments, but we also observe governments "offloading" traditionally governmental functions to NGOs. A problem arises, though, in finding ways to make NGOs accountable for their actions.

Among the hierarchical institutions that have been weakened by the information revolution, the argued, have been traditional political parties. This is reflected in the increased prominence of "celebrity candidates" and "media politics."

Advances in information technology have, of course, contributed to the processes widely recognized as globalization, the speaker noted. Although it is true that trade and investment flows are not a lot greater (in relation to the global economy) than they were in 1900, the speaker argued that harder-to-measure flows of ideas, people, cultural attitudes, etc. are much greater today than they have ever been. He expressed doubts about the significance of the "clashing civilizations" suggested by Samuel Huntington, arguing that the important divisions in the future will be between nations, societies, and groups that accept and adapt to globalization and those that do not.

International competition, he asserted, requires national governments to push their citizens to ever-higher levels of human capital. In this regard, he contrasted the recent experience of East Asia, where the educational attainments of non-elites have been notable, and much of Latin America, where education remains confined to the social and political elite. In conclusion, he noted falling birthrates in a number of industrialized countries and the consequent need in some of these countries for imported labor. An increasingly important characteristic of advanced nations and societies, he suggested, would be their ability to deal with the social implications of rising numbers of foreign workers.

Discussion

In the general discussion that followed these remarks, several participants took issue with a number of the speaker's assertions.

- Questions were raised, for example, about the meaningfulness of statements concerning the "information content" of economic output; information has always been essential to production and at all levels of development. A more sophisticated set of concepts and measurement techniques may be required to capture the true character and extent of changes that are being brought by the information revolution.

- Others participants doubted that the alleged non-accountability of NGOs is a serious problem. Why not stress, they asked, the non-accountability of large private-sector firms?

- Yet others argued that, although the importance of informal communication in networked organizations cannot be doubted, this does not necessarily imply a need for physical proximity. The whole point of improved communication, they argued, is to allow distant individuals to approximate the relationship shared by people meeting face to face.

One participant called for more consideration of how improved communications is changing the way that individuals spend their time and what the social consequences of these changes might be. He argued that a key characteristic of these changes is that today, to a larger degree than previously, people can truly choose how to do their work, live their lives, and spend their time. This participant also asked for more thinking about the degree to which the information revolution has increased the transparency of government operations and about the consequences of this increased transparency.

By the end of the discussion a general consensus had arisen that, although the information revolution has been enabled by technology, its course and its consequences will not be fundamentally determined by technological developments. The course of the information revolution will be driven primarily by social factors.

3. The Technology Underpinnings for the Information Revolution

Speakers: Robert Anderson and Larry Press
Rapporteur: C. Richard Neu

The next session of the conference was devoted to a discussion of potentially important technological developments during the next twenty years, and remarks regarding "information revolution demographics"--who is being affected by the information revolution and how.

Information Technology Trends

The first speaker began by noting that we can be certain that some important technological trends will continue. Computers will continue to get faster, smaller, and cheaper, for example. Wide bandwidth will become increasingly available. The really challenging questions, however, have to do with how businesses and societies will make use of these technological "raw material" to create applications, products, and services that will change people's lives.

Forecasts of such things have been wildly off the mark in the past, and considerable humility is required in this sort of exercise. Nonetheless, this speaker suggested, it is worth thinking about possible future "inflection points"-- the moments that mark dramatic changes in the ways that technology is used. He also warned against focusing too intently on hardware or software trends. True "inflection points" are created by the interaction of technology and society. It wasn't the automobile itself that has turned out to be so important, for example. The changes that have really mattered, he argued, have been the growth of suburbs, the isolation of "nuclear" families in suburban houses physically distant from other generations of the same family, the dependence of industrialized nations on a few Middle Eastern oil producers, and so on.

The speaker identified a number of likely advances in *hardware* that may contribute to important inflection points. The most dramatic and socially significant advances in computing power may be those that arise from the internetting of millions of computers, in effect making the capacity of supercomputers available to anyone with a modem. Some alternatives to current silicon-based electronics may also hold promise for information processing and storage in specialized applications. Among those that might prove workable in the next twenty years are: photonics, DNA computing, nanotubes, quantum computing, and holographic memory devices.

The continuing miniaturization of silicon-based electronics may lead to a proliferation of small and inexpensive sensors during the next twenty years-- with possibly profound social and life-style consequences. The speaker suggested that we may see:

- Ubiquitous miniature television cameras linked to the Internet;

- Smart house, offices, businesses or even cities that would "know" where you are and what you are doing;

- Small sensors with "insect-like" capabilities to crawl, hop, or fly;

- Combinations of information technology and bio-technology to create sensors to detect certain chemicals, drugs, smells, etc. or perhaps to create "body area networks" that monitor and report on a variety of health status indicators.

Significant advances in *software* may be made possible by more automated programming techniques or through "genetic programming" that allows programs to "evolve" in order to solve complex problems. Early efforts to reverse-engineer human sensory organs and parts of the human brain are also showing some promise.

Knowledgeable observers have been (prematurely) forecasting dramatic developments in *artificial intelligence applications* for years. The forecasts may soon be proven correct, the speaker suggested, if only because we will be to apply immense amounts of computing power to these very difficult problems. The applications with the most potential for changing the way people live may be:

- "Good-enough" speech recognition;

- "Good-enough" text understanding to enable effective language translation;

- "Good-enough" pattern recognition to allow automated monitoring of, say, television images;

- And much more capable information retrieval capabilities--perhaps advanced 'bots to search many available sources.

Continued development of communications links may make possible coordinated actions on a massive scale as tens of thousands of Net users organize and coordinate actions--for good or ill. There is every reason to expect that e-commerce will continue its recent growth, increasing competition and squeezing the margins earned by middlemen. Increased "mining" of data generated in everyday life transactions is already proving valuable to some businesses and worrying to some who fear the loss of personal privacy.

Advanced communications technologies may allow rapidly configurable collaborative environments--virtual laboratories, institutes or universities. Also possible may be realistic real-time interactive gaming and simulation environments, allowing much expanded "experience" with complex procedures and situations.

This speaker concluded his remarks by suggesting that the most far-reaching consequences of the information revolution might arise from the fact that it enables other revolutions--especially a revolution in biotechnology.

General discussion of this topic was deferred until after the next presentation.

Information Revolution Demographics

These remarks were followed by some comments on "information revolution demographics"--who is being affected by the information revolution and how. The second speaker noted two principal themes for his remarks: 1) Connectivity to and use of the Internet is spreading very rapidly, but 2) very large disparities in access and use persist.

Almost every country in the world today has some Internet connectivity, he noted. But in many countries, access is very restricted--to small numbers of individuals working in favored institutions in the capital city. Also, bandwidth available for international communication is very limited in many developing countries. The speaker noted that some countries have a total capacity for international Internet communications that is less than is typical for a medium-sized U.S. firm with a T1 line. High-speed connectivity today exists almost exclusively between the United States and Europe and between the United States and Asia. There are very few high-speed links to or among developing economies. About half of all Internet users today are in the United States and Canada.

Internet hosts are heavily concentrated in the United States, Western Europe, and in some parts of Asia. The distribution of the hosts is roughly in line with relative standards of living throughout the world. The number of Internet hosts per capita in a country, for example, shows a strong correlation with the Human Development Indicators monitored by the United Nations Development Program (UNDP).

The last few years have, of course, seen a rapid growth in the number of Web servers. Interestingly, there has been even faster growth in the number of *secure* Web servers. English is by far the dominant language of the Web, and it is even more dominant on secure Web pages.

The speaker warned against thinking about Internet diffusion only in terms of the number of users in a particular country. He suggested six dimensions that characterize the extent of Internet development in a country:

- pervasiveness: a measure based on users per capita and the degree to which non-technicians are using the Internet.

- geographic dispersion: a measure of the concentration of the Internet within a nation, from none or a single city to nationwide availability.

- sectoral absorption: a measure of the degree of utilization of the Internet in the education, commercial, health care and public sectors.

- connectivity infrastructure: a measure based on national and international backbone bandwidth, exchange points, and last-mile access methods.

- organizational infrastructure: a measure based on the state of the ISP industry and market conditions.

- sophistication of use: a measure characterizing usage from conventional to highly sophisticated and driving innovation.

This speaker concluded with a proposal for much more extensive data collection on the use of the Internet, computers, and other information technologies and communications technologies worldwide.

Discussion

The general discussion of this presentation and the preceding one on technology trends began with a question about what, if anything, made information technology different from other advanced technologies. For example, the questioner noted, worldwide patterns of Internet usage are not obviously different from the patterns of clean water, vaccinations, high-quality housing, and many other indicators of standards of living. The second speaker responded that it is largely "a matter of faith"--widely believed but certainly not proved--

that information technology is unique in the possibilities it offers for changing societies. Another participant argued that the Internet is different from other advanced technologies in that its rate of mass adoption has been much faster than any previous technology.

Another participant noted that in both of the preceding presentations we had heard much about *quantities* of information or communication, but almost nothing about the *quality* of this information. The author of the presentation on technology trends suggested that there is probably little to be said about the quality or content of information and communications. The market will out. These media will carry and process whatever information users desire to be carried. Technology, he argued, is neutral with regard to quality.

Another participant noted that correlations between Internet usage and economic factors may be spurious. In many countries, she argued, there is excess capacity within national telephone systems. The real constraints on Internet access and usage, she suggested, are governmental and regulatory. Another participant noted the importance of institutional and legal barriers to Internet use in some countries. The presenter of the material on Internet demographics agreed with these observations, but warned against believing that simple deregulation would be a cure-all.

Other participants pointed to the need for much finer-grained analyses of Internet usage. Our traditional socio-demographic categories may not be adequate for these analyses, one suggested. For example, some of the heaviest and most sophisticated users of the Internet are young people with very low current incomes but access to Internet services through their schools, employers, or families. Another contested the notion that Internet diffusion has proceeded faster than had the diffusion of other technologies; television, he asserted, reached a mass audience more quickly than the Internet has. He also suggested that in some countries and for some demographic groups, the Internet may be substituting for other, still underdeveloped information technologies, and that consequently the diffusion of Internet technology is something of a special case. He also pointed out that the business models of firms that offer Internet technology and services are different in important ways from the business models of firms offering other technologies and services. Until we understand these business models and their implications, we will not fully understand what drives or retards diffusion of the Internet. Yet another participant noted that treatment of intellectual property rights may also have much to do with the way in which the Internet is utilized in different countries.

Near the end of the discussion, a number of participants expressed some impatience with the concentration on who uses the Internet and how much. They argued for more attention to the political and social consequences of using this or any other information technology. In this connection, another participant introduced terminology that proved useful throughout the rest of the conference. He distinguished between "technology"--the know-how or understanding that allows us to accomplish particular ends--and the "artifacts"--the actual applications--that we build with our technology. He argued that the artifacts will be of much greater political and social consequence than will the technology itself.

Part II.

Various Dimensions of the Information Revolution

4. The Political/Governmental Dimension of the Information Revolution

Moderator: David Gompert

Speakers: William Drake and Paul Bracken

Rapporteur: Richard Hundley

The next session of the conference discussed the political/governmental dimension of the information revolution. It focused primarily on possible changes in the role of the nation state as a result of the information revolution. It began with two speakers, followed by an audience discussion.

The Information Revolution, National Sovereignty, and Political Change

The first speaker began by listing three guiding principles that should be followed in any discussion of the impact of the information revolution on national sovereignty, and resulting political change:

- We should avoid technology determinism. Technology by itself does not tell the whole story.

- We should not ignore sources of continuity. There are many operating in the geopolitical realm.

- We need to develop careful comparative research.

He went on to note that this is not the first time national sovereignty has been called into question. Rather, national sovereignty has been viewed as challenged by each new communication media. What is new about the Internet is the distributed nature of access and content.

The speaker listed two different aspects of sovereignty:

- Constitutional sovereignty: the legal authority and primacy of national governments within their territorial domains.[5]

- Operational sovereignty: the ability of governments to exercise effective control within their territorial domains.

Constitutional sovereignty is not being challenged by the information revolution. But operational sovereignty is, both technically and with regard to cost.

The speaker noted that the current political science literature addressing the impact of the information revolution on international and national politics is posed mainly in black-and-white terms: <u>either</u> the nation state is on the way out, <u>or</u> the nation state is as powerful as ever. He feels that the situation is not either-or, but rather somewhere in between, and varies from state to state.

At the conclusion of this talk, an associate of the speaker noted that various writers have suggested that the Internet is a force for democratization (i.e., for political change in authoritarian societies). Whether or not this is true in any given country depends, in his view, on four "Internet and democratization variables":

- Regulation strategy

- Openness of the political system

- A state's vulnerability to international pressure

- The level of economic liberalization in a regime.

The Role of Nationalism in the Information Revolution

According to the second speaker, a current widely held view is that nationalism -- which he defines as a shared identity and feelings of attachment among the citizens of a nation -- should decline in importance because of globalization. He does not agree with this view. Rather, he believes that nationalism is on the rise in many parts of the world, particularly in Asia. He acknowledges that nationalism may be a somewhat declining force in North America and Western Europe, but believes it to be a rising force in many Asian nations (e.g., India, China, etc.)

----

[5] The speaker also referred to this as "Westphalian sovereignty," in reference to the Treaty of Westphalia in 1648, at the conclusion of the Thirty Years' War, which established the principle that nation states do not interfere in the internal affairs of other nation states.

According to the speaker, nationalism has a bad reputation in political science today. It often gets equated with labels like "xenophobic," "extreme,", etc. This may be because governments often have manipulated nationalist feelings to obtain results that they could not otherwise achieve.

But nationalism can be put to positive, progressive uses as well. For example, the Asian nations tapped forces of nationalism during the 1920s – 1950s to through out their colonial rulers and achieve independence. Today, according to the speaker, the only way for a nation like Russia to modernize is to harness nationalism. Russian, and other, leaders can use nationalism as a counter to the centrifugal forces of globalization, which threaten to break up many nations.

The speaker noted that we are at a time of rapid economic change in the world. This implies higher levels of "creative destruction" and resulting disruption. In many cases these lead to a decline in real security (e.g., as obtained from job, religion, community), especially among the lower and middle classes. Nationalism will often serve to counter this.

The speaker also noted that just as we need to study nationalism to understand world history over the last 150 years, he believes that nationalism will be equally relevant in the future.

For all of the above reasons, the speaker believes that the U.S. should not become, or be seen as, the "enemy of nationalism."

The Discussion

The moderator began the discussion portion of this session by noting that in considering the political/governmental impacts of the information revolution, we should be careful to look at "more or less," not just "yes or no." (In other words, things are not just black and white, but have many varying shades of gray.) Secondly, we should be careful about assigning causality, since there are other major causes operating today, not just cheaper and better information technology. Thirdly, we need to consider direct versus indirect effects.

Several participants responded to the nationalism theme raised by the second speaker. One noted that nationalism serves as an important filter through which many people interpret the information they receive via the Internet and other media; for example, CNN and the New York Times are not seen as "neutral" by many non-U.S. viewers/readers. Another participant stated that some nations (such as India) are linking technology to nationalism, to further the course of the information revolution in their country. Still another participant suggested we consider how nationalism will play out in the information age between information revolution "haves" -- e.g., between the U.S. and Canada, or between England and Scotland.

Another participant posed the question: in the world at large (i.e., outside of the U.S.), to what extent is IT and the information revolution seen as another U.S. "threat" (i.e., of increasing U.S. hegemony)? This seemed to strike a positive chord with several participants:

- One non-U.S. participant stated that the Internet is seen as an expression of U.S. nationalism by most of the rest of the world, regardless of whether it's being used deliberately as such by the U.S.

- Another non-U.S. participant noted that in 1997 there was US Congressional testimony stating that more than 70% of the value of information products worldwide was of US origin. Also, the same participant noted, the possibility that US law on commerce (especially in cyberspace) will dominate against other legal norms is being debated in Congress.

- In response, a U.S. participant noted that many in the U.S. would view the U.S. approach to IT, the Internet, and the information revolution not as a manifestation of <u>nationalism</u>, but rather of <u>internationalism</u> -- specifically, an extension of the belief that our ideas, especially involving democracy, are perhaps the only basis for legitimacy. He went on to suggest that those in the U.S. having this view are very narrow-minded.

- A second U.S. participant agreed with the characterization of this view (i.e., that the U.S. is internationalist rather than nationalist in its approach to the Internet and the information revolution) as narrow-minded. He stated his belief that U.S. nationalism is very strong, saying that we mask it as "human rights," democracy," etc., but have a strong affinity for the U.S. "model" or "role."

Another participant noted that, historically, nationalism has been based on geographical communities. The Internet makes possible non-geographic, network communities. These network communities can be either global (i.e., larger than nations) or local (i.e., smaller than nations). As the information revolution progresses, these network communities may come to suppliant, at least partially, communities based on nationalism.

Changing the subject (somewhat), still another participant posed the question: who will be the "Jimmy Hoffa" of the information age? That is, what if someone organizes the system administrators of the world? If so, will he control the information revolution?

Another participant noted that the empowerment of individuals (e.g., Osama bin Laden) through the use of information technology is a new political factor brought into being by the information revolution. Several other participants endorsed this comment, emphasizing the importance of this factor.

The moderator ended the discussion by noting that we should not forget the contribution of information technology to "hard power."

5. The Business/Financial Dimension of the Information Revolution

Moderator: C. Richard Neu
Speakers: Jim Norton and Colin Crook
Rapporteur: Richard Hundley

The next session of the conference was devoted to a discussion of the business and financial dimension of the information revolution. It focused in particular on two aspects of IT-driven changes in the business and financial world: electronic commerce, and new models for the internal organization and functioning of business enterprises and for their external interactions with customers, suppliers, and competitors.

Electronic Commerce

The first speaker discussed electronic commerce, using recent developments in the United Kingdom as a point of departure.[6]

Why E-Commerce Is Important

As viewed by the speaker, electronic commerce is important for several reasons:

* *Its dramatic growth and potential.* According to the speaker, the speed of adoption of e-commerce is unprecedented. While electronic data interchange between large companies has developed steadily over the last fifteen years, there has recently been an explosion of growth in retail e-commerce and in transactional use by small business.

  Industry forecasts have consistently underestimated e-commerce growth. In the U.S. business to business e-commerce is now expected to reach $1 trillion

---

[6] See Cabinet Office (1999) for a detailed discussion of the UK e-commerce vision and program.

by 2003. Similarly, business to consumer e-commerce is thought to have reached $7 billion in 1998 and to be on track to reach between $40 billion and $80 billion by 2002. This suggests that the current pattern, where at least 80% of e-commerce revenues fall in the business-to-business segment, is being maintained. In the UK, e-commerce revenues are expected to reach $4.5 billion for 1999, rising to $47 billion by 2002.

- *The major impact it will have on barriers to market entry.* E-commerce demolishes many existing market barriers, including geographic and market separation barriers (e.g., products and services available in one country but not in another, for a variety of reasons), custom and practice barriers (e.g., products and services sold only through intermediaries, such as travel agents, etc.), and business scale barriers (e.g., the ease with which small e-commerce start-ups can quickly become major players in an established market, such as Amazon.com in book-selling).

- *The way it enables increased efficiency and effectiveness within existing business models.* The speaker gave several examples of UK companies that were able to reduce development costs and shorten product development cycles by means of e-commerce links to their suppliers. In the business-to-consumer area, he gave additional examples of U.S. companies that improved productivity, reduced cost, and increased customer satisfaction by means of e-commerce.

- Most importantly, *the way it enables transformation of existing business models.* [7] E-commerce is transforming business, by reducing transaction costs (resulting in improved efficiencies and new business opportunities), breaking down geographical barriers (yet with a premium on "clusters" of tacit knowledge), and accelerating rates of change.

Besides its impact on business, E-commerce is also affecting governments and people in fundamental ways. It affects *government* by increasing efficiency and changing interactions with the outside world, affecting the speed and availability of information, and challenging existing regulatory frameworks. It affects *people* by reducing prices, creating new products and services and increasing choice, changing working methods, and, on the negative side, by creating possibilities of social exclusion.

----

[7] The second speaker addressed this in more detail.

Stages in E-Commerce Adoption: Offshore Out-Sourcing versus Clusters

According to the speaker, *stage one* of e-commerce adoption usually focuses on cost reduction via increased efficiencies and effectiveness within existing business models. This often tends to attract companies offshore, to areas with:

- Lower labor costs, yet a high standard of education.

- Good (local) infrastructure with global connectivity,

- Tax breaks for exports.

This ignores the impact of *stage two* of e-commerce, which involves revolutionary change in the business model. This requires skills in innovation and business change that are likely to be incompatible with offshore out-sourcing. Such skills are more likely to be found in "clusters": geographic concentrations of interconnected companies and institutions in a particular field.[8]

According to the speaker, the balance between these two forces, offshore out-sourcing and clusters, will have a crucial impact on European economies, particularly for immaterial products or services.

The UK Vision Regarding E-Commerce

As described by the speaker, the UK government has the following vision for where it wants the UK to be with regard to e-commerce in 2002:

For individuals:

- A higher percentage of people in the UK will have access to e-commerce networks from home than in any other G7 country;

- The total cost of Internet access will be lower in the UK than in any other G7 country;

- A higher percentage of the population will use multi-function smartcards than in any other G7 country.

For business:

- A higher percentage of business-to-business and business-to-consumer transactions will be carried out on e-commerce networks than in any other G7 country.

----

[8] See Porter (1998) for a discussion of such "clusters."

For Government:

- A higher percentage of total government services may be transacted through E-commerce networks than in any other G7 country.

The UK government has identified three *pillars* on which the achievement of this vision must be based:

- *Understanding:* The need to create awareness of opportunities and threats posed by e-commerce, overcoming uncertainty and imperfect information about electronic markets, and breaking down skill barriers.
- *Access:* Giving business and individuals the ability to interact, thereby accelerating the achievement of critical mass in electronic markets.
- *Trust:* Giving consumers (business and individual) confidence in electronic markets and ensuring that they are willing to exploit the opportunities and react to the threats.

The UK government has identified a number of barriers to achieving this vision in 2002, including: an environment in the UK insufficiently competitive, entrepreneurial, and innovative to force e-commerce adoption throughout industry; inadequate coordination and focus of e-commerce initiatives across government; lack of internationally agreed-upon fiscal and regulatory frameworks for e-commerce; and inadequate monitoring of e-commerce outcomes. According to the speaker, the UK government has agreed on a set of actions to overcome these barriers, strengthen the three pillars, and attain the vision.[9]

New Business Models Driven by the Information Revolution

The second speaker discussed new models for the internal organization and functioning of business enterprises, and for their external interactions with customers, suppliers, and competitors.

He began by noting that skepticism exists in some quarters that things are really different.[10] After all, businesses have been bombarded by waves of "fads" over the decades. Could the information revolution be just another fad?

----

[9] As indicated earlier, Cabinet Office (1999) discusses all aspects of this UK e-commerce program.

[10] The speaker characterized these skeptics as "economists," as distinguished from "financial journalists and investment advisors," who (apparently) in his view are not skeptics.

In his view, emerging evidence suggests that things are indeed different. The present is a time of great experimentation in the business world, with lots of data emerging. It represents an unique opportunity for testing old and new models and theories.

The Changing Environment for Business

Today, the global IT grid, with "free" communications, total connectivity, universal digitization, pervasive influence, and vast data generation, is a driver of fundamental change in the business world. These changes include:

- Globalization, of more and more business and financial activities.
- Changes in scale, with the new information technology allowing a company to focus on one person, or on one billion people.
- Non-linear and positive-feedback effects, frequently including a large "first mover" advantage.
- Accelerating rates of change, with speed and time becoming critical in business ventures.
- Emerging new social structures, in which businesses much exist and function.
- Loss of conventional reference frameworks.

These changes are leading to a "new era economics," characterized by a knowledge economy, non-linear effects, an unpredictable future, a redefinition of terms, time/distance changes, and much greater transparency (in pricing and other aspects of business).

As a result of all of this, many fundamental tenets of business are being questioned. Since most businesses today are not externally focussed -- in the speaker's view -- making sense of these changes becomes a serious problem.

The New Business Model

This changing environment is leading to a new business model, with the following major elements:

- Centrality of the <u>customer</u>; the dominant factor in business today, influencing everything.[11]

- A <u>non-linear world</u> defining business processes; business capabilities must explicitly address this.

- <u>Competition's</u> fundamental role, forcing continuing adaptation and change.

- A <u>services/capabilities</u> approach to developing everything.

- <u>Globalization</u>.

- <u>Technology and business</u> integrated into a unified approach.

- A <u>continuum</u> of individual/enterprise/community/NGOs/government/ nations; businesses must handle this continuum.

- <u>Redefined</u> basic functions of business.

The speaker gave a number of examples of the *Rules* in this new business model, including:

- Businesses must be externally driven.

- Businesses must adapt, not optimize.

- Businesses explicitly manage risk.

- Businesses must operate in real time.[12]

- Business must be non-linear in their capabilities.

- Businesses must have customer-based loops.[13]

- Businesses cannot plan anymore.[14]

- Businesses must use new paradigms for product, service, delivery, support, and pricing.

- Businesses must regard competition as fundamental to their development and progress.

- Businesses must resolve and exploit the customer paradox (i.e., the ability to focus on one and millions, at the same time).

----

[11] According to the speaker, companies are valued at $200 to $3000 per customer today. This is the main current metric for company valuation.

[12] As example of this rule, the speaker mentioned a large, multinational financial services company which now closes its books every day, rather than once a quarter, as it used to do.

[13] As an example of this rule, the speaker mentioned Microsoft, which shipped out about one million copies of Windows 2000 for beta test and debugging; the customer thereby becoming an integral part of the Microsoft business model.

[14] In the sense of detailed, long-term strategic plans that have any enduring utility. As an example of this, the same multinational financial services company mentioned previously no longer develops a five-year strategic plan or annual budgets.

- Businesses must use true innovation as the basis for breaking the dominance of increasing returns (i.e., positive feedback).[15]

- Businesses must discover the key shaping forces for self-organization.

- Businesses must change the connectivity from the supply chain to the customer.[16]

Some Key Examples of Change

The speaker gave some key examples of change occurring as a result of this new business model and its new rules:

- A revolution is in process in pricing, with prices becoming much more dynamic, often determined in auctions, frequently personalized to target individual customers, and much more transparent.

- Information from the real world, rather than the internal, company world, increasingly drives business. This leads to many issues and problems (e.g., privacy, control, transparency, authenticity, making sense of all the information, etc.).

- Business is increasingly coupled to the real-time world. The worldwide financial community is a good example of this; all of its systems are tuned to the real-time world.

- New forms of marketing are shaping self-organization of businesses.

- The customer is becoming the co-producer of the business.[17]

Based on all of the above, the speaker believes that things are indeed different; lots of evidence suggests that new things are taking place in the economy, with science and technology beginning to dominate business. Businesses cannot afford to wait; they must participate now. Some outlines are already in place to show them the way (e.g. the rules listed above).

These changes look profound and disturbing to some (in the business world and elsewhere), but the business community and the broader society are beginning to adapt. All of this leads, among other things, to a new and interesting stress between the individual and government.

----

[15] According to the speaker, much of company valuation these days is based on the concept of increasing returns of scale, and bets on who will dominate. (But many will fail.)

[16] Walmart and Amazon.com are two well known examples of companies that have done this.

[17] Microsoft's involvement of its customers in the beta testing of its software, mentioned above, is an example of this.

The speaker concluded by saying that businesses changed dramatically during the 1980s and 1990s, but he believes that even more profound change is in prospect. The "new era ethos" is "to participate and experience business reality."

The Discussion

In the general discussion that followed these remarks, one participant cited the varying structures of capital markets in different nations as an important differential determinant of the future course of the information revolution. According to this participant, the availability of funding for new IT businesses and concepts and the manner of the funding process (i.e., the vagaries of getting funding, listings, capital, acquisitions, etc.) directly impact the growth and development of new IT industries in any given region. She views this as critical because, in her words, new Internet concepts/businesses are anti-establishment by their very nature -- they upset and challenge the old business models, monopolies and ways of doing things -- and yet money is a very establishment thing in most countries. She believes that the free and open flow of capital, the existence of seed and venture capital, and vibrant over-the-counter markets like NASDAQ (which give venture capitalists and start-up employees an exit market) are critical enabling factors for the growth and proliferation of IT.

The ability of start-ups to get such funding differs greatly from one nation to another. For example, she cited Taiwan as a nation that aggressively uses equity financing for start-ups.[18] Hong Kong and Singapore, on the other hand, lack a strong equity culture and a secondary market, and rely much more heavily on debt financing. But debt financing requires a track record and punishes failure -- both of which are detrimental to start-ups.

In this participant's view, equity participation for most/all members of the staff of an IT start-up (the current Silicon Valley model) facilitates the attraction of top people.[19] This is something else you lose with debt financing.

Returning to the new business model described by the second speaker, another participant noted that the ability to have real-time, 24-hour business information (e.g., "closing the books" once a day) will be transforming for businesses. They

---

[18] According to this participant, in this regard Taiwan is very similar to Silicon Valley.

[19] In Silicon Valley today, this use of equity shares in lieu of salary, etc. extends well beyond the staffs of the start-ups themselves. Many of the accounting and law firms providing services to start-ups are accepting equity shares in lieu of fees.

will have much better information on which to base decisions (as opposed, for example, to the information available from a quarterly closing of the books).

This participant also noted the large data sets (of customer information, etc.) becoming available because of IT. He stated that some businesses have been able to extract "amazing" business-relevant value from these data sets.

Finally, another participant noted that various studies exist of "national innovation systems." He suggested that these studies should have some relevance to the current discussion.[20]

----

[20] See Nelson (1993) for a discussion of one such study of national innovation systems.

6. The Social/Cultural Dimension of the Information Revolution

Moderator: Tora Bikson
Speaker: Jon Alterman
Rapporteur: Jerrold Green

The Presentation

This section of the conference was devoted to a discussion of the socio-cultural implications of the information revolution. The speaker hypothesized that the information revolution is likely to bring with it significant change and unrest, particularly within the developing areas which were his primary focal point. In particular, it was argued that technology tends to exacerbate differences within a society, while at the same time facilitating the mobilization of those who remain what he termed "non-infocentric." The information revolution is likely to be significant for U.S. foreign policy-makers as political stability is certain to be exacerbated by the increasing salience of social conditions and problems. The challenge to national elites, as well as to U.S. policymakers, will be to manage the transition towards info-centric decision-making, given the concomitant social and cultural tensions that it is likely to create.

According to the speaker, one outgrowth of the information revolution is globalization. He identifies the core elements of globalization as:

* more information flowing with less obstruction

* information flowing independent of distance

* increasing opportunities for economic cooperation across borders

* greater opportunities to profit globally.

According to the speaker, there are two especially popular models of the implications of the information revolution. The first he termed the "Golden Straightjacket," which has been popularized by Thomas Friedman, in which economic development is regarded as a primary driver to socio-political change. This varies from a parallel perspective, popularized by Samuel Huntington, in which as a result of the "clash of civilizations," culture, rather than economic development, is the primary driver to change. Rejecting both concepts as being somewhat too static, the speaker presented a third possibility in which he asserted that economic unrest can take cultural forms, and that an over-emphasis on Western consumerism, coupled with hostility towards Westernized elites, can exacerbate even further the cultural dimensions of this conflict.

In looking at the convergence of cultural and economic stimuli to unrest, outgrowths of the information revolution as understood by the speaker, he then shifted his attention to what he termed the globalization of information. Here he sees the following phenomena in play:

- the erosion of censorship

- people being inundated with vast quantities of information

- the democratization of information

- the empowerment of the individual through access to increased information.

In order to sustain these assertions, the author provided a number of examples, virtually all of which were from the Middle East. This emphasis on one region, at the expense of others, raised a number of questions in the ensuing discussion. These are dealt with below.

In an attempt to explore further the intertwining of cultural and economic forces as part of the information revolution, the speaker then turned his attention to what he termed the "globalization of style." Here he talked about a variety of entertainment products, fashion and brand names, and so forth. The globalization of style tends to be largely an American inspired phenomenon making the U.S. a particularly salient target for political dissent and resentment. Such products as Coca Cola, Baywatch, Michael Jordan, and other commodities tend to be American in content and character, and the single biggest national purveyor of this globalization of style is clearly the United States, which may be challenged because of this.

The speaker emphasized the degree to which English-language literacy is synonymous with the globalization of information. This is the case not only in terms of hardware acquisition, installation, and repair, but also in the realm of software applications. The dominance of the English language in the global information revolution is accompanied by what he termed the bombardment of

Western images. He asserted that the prevalence of Western images is both tempting and frustrating, as it may create unattainable desires.

An additional element of the global information revolution is increased social stratification in which those most likely to participate most actively tend to have fluency in English, foreign ties, and high degrees of education. Thus, the speaker asserted that the information revolution is a phenomenon that is largely restricted to the political elite. He further asserted that only a limited group can afford to acquire high-tech devices, and that a relatively small group profits economically from the information revolution. Indeed, in some place the market for these tools is already saturated.

The result of this skewed global information revolution is further societal divisions, with a technologically savvy, highly educated, and IT conversant elite juxtaposed with a technologically unsophisticated, undereducated group of people which has been passed over by the information revolution. At the same time, the speaker noted that there is the spread of low-cost, low-tech devices, such as photocopiers, telephones, fax, videotapes, and the like, which both facilitate communication and are more broadly inclusive. It is his view that the growth of such technology facilitates mobilization for political dissent, both within borders and across them. He further noted that unless states continue to rely on a strong state model, their sovereignty will erode in large part due to facilitated trans-border as well as internal communications which are beyond the control of the state. The consequences of this within societies are:

- greater awareness of prosperity elsewhere and poverty at home
- desires among some for greater "cultural authenticity"
- a growing gap between rich and poor
- empowerment of individuals vis-à-vis their governments
- gradual adaptation to a surplus of information.

The speaker concluded his presentation by talking about how the globalization of information exacerbates societal cleavages and is likely to destabilize some governments. He further noted that it aids trans-national movements, creates new sources of authority, and widens socio-political gaps. If current trends persist, we can expect to see more political movements using IT as an element of political dissent, a flattening curve of IT growth, a growing hostility toward political elites in a number of settings, and increasing alienation in a number of sectors.

The speaker concluded by recommending that human capacity in key countries be fostered as the benefits of the information revolution must be distributed more equitably. He also asserted that we must understand neo-traditionalist movements as modern, not regressive. The case he clearly had in mind here were Islamic groups, which are regarded in the West as being backward-looking, when in fact he believes they are forward-looking. As a foreign policy consideration, the United States and its allies must be prepared for instability as certain regimes friendly to the U.S. are likely to become collateral victims to an information revolution, which he regards as having a significant ability to destabilize.

The Discussion

In the general discussion that followed these remarks, a number of participants took issue with several of the speaker's assertions.

- One participant argued that the presentation's emphasis on the negative and destructive aspects of the information revolution was simply inaccurate. The speaker was challenged to provide examples beyond the Middle East; another participant responded with examples from South America.

- Another participant suggested that IT penetration outside the Middle East is on a far greater scale, and is not restricted exclusively to elites.[21] She also challenged the presenter's assertion that the information revolution was primarily an English-language phenomenon, and that, indeed, throughout Asia, materials in local languages are available for the operation of computers, software, and the like..

- Another participant took issue with the notion that those being excluded from the information revolution wish to opt out of it. He suggested that the have-nots are as eager to be embraced by the information revolution as are those at its core. He cited examples from under-developed countries and elsewhere.

- Another speaker from the floor suggested that we must be careful in discussing the role of "language." Linguistic problems and uses differ significantly from hardware, to email, to web pages, to user manuals, and so forth. Thus, different sectors offer different linguistic challenges.

----

[21] Another participant, however, suggested Africa may resemble the Middle East in low IT penetration rates.

- It was suggested that much of what the speaker said seemed to focus primarily on the Internet, without paying adequate attention to satellite television, telephony, and the like.

- On speaker noted with approval that the presentation highlighted the difficulties in generalizing across cultures.

- This assertion was challenged by another participant, who talked about the efforts of a global financial institution which found striking consistencies amongst customers worldwide, and that cultural differences in some areas at least may be far less significant than one might think.

- Another speaker talked about the role of "good information" and "bad information" and suggested that just as economic markets allow for the survival of some things and the demise of others, that good information will prevail while bad information will disappear.

The discussion concluded with a general recognition that generalizations about the cultural and social dimensions of the information revolution are exceedingly difficult to formulate. While there are certain universalities which were identified, there are also regional and national peculiarities which are not always that easy to ascertain. The information revolution will continue to be driven by a complex intermingling of political, social, cultural, and economic factors. It is by understanding the intermingling of these factors that we can begin to understand and anticipate the future of the information revolution.

Part III.

How the Information Revolution May Proceed Differently in Various Regions of the World

7. Three National/Regional Snapshots

Speakers: Hideo Miyashita, V. S. Arunachalam, and Ernest Wilson
Rapporteur: Richard Hundley

The conference began its discussion of the different ways in which the information revolution may proceed in various regions of the world by considering three national/regional snapshots: Japan, India, and Africa. It then separated into breakout groups for in-depth discussions of different regions.

This section covers the three national/regional snapshots. Section 8 (North, Central, and South America), Section 9 (Europe), Section 10 (the Asia Pacific region), and Section 11 (Middle East, Africa, and South Asia) present the results of the breakout group discussions.

The Present Status and Characteristics of the Information Revolution in Japan

The first speaker began by presenting his image of the development of the information society, as a whole, that has occurred and will eventually occur in all countries. In his view, the first phase of the information society started around 1990 when PCs were first connected by networks, especially by the Internet.[22] At this point, computers changed their main function from information processing machines to network terminals, with people using the network for information gathering and communication. The network covers individuals as well as small offices and is changing the way we conduct business as well as our lifestyles.

----

[22] This first phase of the information society, beginning roughly in 1990, was preceded by a 20 to 30 year period during which the computerization of society occurred. During this time, computers were used primarily for information processing, leading to increased efficiencies of business activities mainly in big companies and organizations.

Now, according to the speaker, the second phase of the information society is beginning: some people are saying good-bye to their PCs. Within 5-10 years, fixed PC networks will be replaced by multi-media networks that will enable broad-band communications and various mobile digitized services. Finally, the information society will reach the third and final stage: an ubiquitous network that will come into being within 20 years, enabling everything to be connected to the network.

The speaker then presented a variety of statistical information regarding the current status and characteristics of the Japanese information society, including the following:

- As of March 1999, the penetration of IT appliances into Japanese homes (40 million total families) was as follows: PCs, in 29.5% of Japanese homes; PCs connected to the Internet, in 13% of the homes; fax machines, in 26.4% of the homes; VCRs, 77.8%; CD players, 60.1%; video disc players, 15.2%; video cameras, 36.3%; satellite TV receivers, 36.6%; and TV game machines, in more than 50% of the homes. In addition, 40% of the Japanese population have cellular telephones.

- The Internet took only five years to reach 10% penetration of Japanese homes. This compares to the PC, 13 years for 10% penetration; cellular telephones, 15 years; fax machines, 19 years; pagers, 24 years; and telephone service, 76 years to reach 10% penetration of Japanese homes.

- The Internet revolution in Japan started in 1995, when commercial use of the Internet began and Windows 95 was put on the market. The number of people who use the Internet from the office, school, and home has jumped from 4 million in March 1996 to 17 million in March 1999 (40% of the population). Although the use of the Internet first occurred in big business organizations and the central government, as of March, 1999, the number of home users slightly surpassed that of office and school users.

- Internet shopping companies first appeared in Japan in 1995. Their number is increasing rapidly, from about 100 in December 1995 to about 7000 in December 1997, and to about 18000 in October 1999. The total size of the Japanese business-to-consumer e-commerce market in 1998 was about 17 billion Yen. The business-to-business e-commerce market was much larger, about 243 billion Yen.

Reflecting on these statistics, the speaker said that the Internet is becoming a necessity for young high-school and college students, as well as for the average businessman. During the last 5 years, most big Japanese companies, central and local governmental organizations, and major non-profit organizations have launched home pages on the Internet. Most Japanese industries are very anxious now to introduce the Internet and extranets into their business structures, for functions such as supply chain management or marketing. The Internet is now becoming a kind of infrastructure for Japanese industries and society. These drastic changes have taken place over only 4-5 years. The Japanese people are now recognizing that they are experiencing an "Internet Revolution" or "Digital Information Revolution."

The speaker then summarized the results of a recent international survey of people's attitudes towards the information revolution in four countries: Japan, the U.S., South Korea, and Singapore.[23]

- Of the four countries, only the Japanese thought that the age of information does not bring about more active interaction and communication among people; a majority of the Americans, Koreans, and Singaporeans thought it did.

- The Japanese were the least anxious of the four about being left behind by the information revolution.

- The Koreans and Americans had the strongest desires for self-expression, and the Koreans were the most positive about having their own web pages. The Japanese ranked last in both of these categories.

- The Japanese have the most negative attitude regarding the use of cellular phones in public places – much more negative than the other three countries.

- The Singaporeans were the most positive regarding having additional TV channels, followed closely by the Koreans. The Japanese and Americans were the least positive.

The speaker then listed a number of characteristics of Japanese society and other factors which he believed may influence the future course of the information revolution in Japan. He classified these factors into accelerating types (i.e., those that will aid the revolution and decelerating types (i.e., those that will hinder the revolution, and he identified which ones impacted the political, business, and social dimensions. His list of factors is shown in Table 7.1

----

[23] This survey was conducted by the Nomura Research Institute at the end of 1997. The sample sizes were 1400 persons in Japan and 500 in each of the other three countries.

Table 7.1

**Characteristics of Japanese Society
Which May Influence the Information Revolution in Japan**

	Political/ Governmental Dimension	Business/Financial Dimension	Social/Cultural Dimension
Accelerating Factors	Strong central government which intends to keep strong leadership of Japanese information society	Highly established industrial structure and powerful companies Hardware appliance-oriented manufacturing industry High scientific and technology level in IT Deregulation of industries Worldwide strength in TV game software and animation industry	Diversified cultural tradition including entertainment Strong upward thinking High level of education (but lacking diversity and flexibility)
Decelerating Factors	Strong central government which may lead to too much standardization and uniformity High population density and centralized land use pattern Population structure in the future (aged people)	Regulations for industry by central and local governments Conservative and passive consumers Traditional practices in the marketing and distribution systems High price level for telecom services	Language barrier Long history of printing culture (paper) Social customs and traditions (e.g., face to face) Strong influence of mass media (centralized TV networks and newspapers) Keyboard phobia Homogeneous and uniform values Not so open society Lack of challenging attitude to change society

Regarding this list, the speaker elaborated on the following four factors which he thought were most important for the future course of the information revolution in Japan:

- The great inertia which Japanese society has regarding its traditional culture, values, and social customs bears considerable emphasis in any discussion of IT-induced change. For example, the Japanese regard face-to-face communication to be of the utmost importance, no matter whether it is for business or for private purposes, or for educational or religions purposes. Commuting by train to the work place and having face-to-face meetings with colleagues or supervisors is still one of the most important customs in Japanese society. Also, Japanese consumers have some tendency to place an emphasis on face-to-face service at shops or financial counters.

  In addition, a sizeable portion of Japanese consumers prefer cash payments and do not use credit cards. Also, Japanese consumers are very cautious when using the Internet for shopping. They hesitate to put their credit card numbers into the open network. The majority of Japanese consumers who have access to the Internet are waiting to see how their risk will be decreased by government regulation or industry standards. As individuals they do not like taking on risk by themselves. They also prefer to maintain the status quo when possible.

  It is true, as the speaker noted, that the passage of 10 to 20 years will change some of those traditional customs that affect the spread of Internet usage. However, he pointed out that the "slow changing society" is deeply rooted in the customs and traditions of Japan. This culture is not likely to change in a short period.

- The impact of regulations and traditional practices within the Japanese market, especially with regard to distribution systems, is another impediment to IT-induced change. There are a number of Japanese industries whose traditional distribution systems are becoming an obstacle to the introduction of Internet-oriented business systems.

  For example, in the case of automobile sales, the existence of a Japanese automobile dealers association, organized by manufactures and area sales agents, builds up some barriers for newcomers. In addition, many Japanese consumers welcome the automobile salesman who makes house-calls. Some Japanese groups and Auto-by-Tel are now trying to challenge and change the structure of this market.

  As another example, the travel service agent industry is obliged by law to sell tickets and services over the counter. The travel agent must employ staff members who have government qualifications at every branch office. The Ministry of Transportation is gradually alleviating these regulations.[24]

In the case of books, the Re-sale Price Maintenance Rule is applied for books in Japan. This means that no one may discount new books and magazines. In addition, the existence of cartel-like distribution networks between book stores and publishing companies makes it difficult for newcomers to enter the market. Many Japanese consumers seem to be satisfied with the neighborhood book stores that are found in every town in Japan. Amazon.com and similar online book sellers have to compete with those small, entrenched book stores that already control the Japanese market

- The speaker's next point dealt with the effect of the Internet on the centralized and uniform media within Japan. Japan has good television networks and good newspapers on the national level.[25] People have been talking about the de-centralization of Japanese society in terms of political, economical, and cultural dimensions for long time. However, the influences of central government, large financial and industrial groups, good universities, and famous cultural and artistic organizations, mostly located in Tokyo, are still very strong. These influences are reinforced by the centralized Japanese news media.

In addition, in Japanese society people tend to put a higher priority on the values of the organization or group rather than on the individual. Clearly, this does not necessarily lead to totalitarianism. Rather, Japanese people do not like to express their opinions clearly or insist on individual beliefs too much. They dislike projecting themselves outside the group, especially in public or formal circumstances. Japanese people value consensus as opposed to open, conflicting discussions.

This characteristic of Japanese society has a good compatibility with television. TV is a mass media that is good for passive people. People can enjoy nationally based, one-way broadcasting services at any time.

However, the Internet is different. Television only requires from the consumer a passive acquiescence to the flickering images on the screen. The Internet requires an active attitude. The user has to think about what he or she wants and then actively engage the various navigation and

----

[24] Many young Japanese businessmen are now using the Internet to reserve airline tickets and hotel rooms. However, they still must pay by separate means.

[25] Of course, there are also local TV stations and newspapers, but most of them are supplementary to their national counterparts.

communication tools required for its gain. It is difficult for inherently passive consumers to recognize the merits of the Internet.

The speaker believes the Internet is a media oriented around de-centralization. This lack of center is the essential nature of Internet as a media. In its ideal form, it will give power to the individual rather than to organizations or central powers. For the moment, the Internet, as a social media, is facing "friction" from those characteristics of Japanese society that guaranteed the success of television.

• Next, the speaker talked about the unique characteristics of the Japanese information technology industry. It is often mentioned that the strength of Japanese industry rests in its ability to develop and manufacture hardware and not in software. The speak believes that this is fundamentally true and will remain true for the next 10 to 20 years.

Although Japan has no Microsoft or Netscape, Japanese electronic companies are now strengthening their power in the market of home information technology appliances. According to the speaker, people in Japan are saying goodbye to their PCs and the market for various home telecom terminals and electronic appliances is becoming far larger. This growth will be accelerated with the advent of even more advanced multimedia networks, and, the speaker believes, will increase even further with the advent of the ubiquitous network age which we will someday achieve. The Japanese electronic industry has traditionally been strong in the home electronic-appliance arena. In the future, they will focus their research and development on the eventual integration of those electronic appliances into the home LAN and mobile networks. This kind of technological emphasis will constitute another strength of the future Japanese information technology industry and will insure its high value in the new market.

Concerning software, some unique software industries are now growing rapidly in Japan, for example, the television or computer game software industry. Together with hardware game-machine manufacturers like Sony, Sega, and Nintendo, many young and creative game software companies with high computer graphics technology are attracting attention internationally. The Japanese animation industries are also trying to digitize their business. These entertainment software industries may be changing into a sort of "Virtual Hollywood" whose market is far larger than the real movie market.

The speaker believes that U.S. companies are stronger in business oriented software or efficiency-improving software, whereas Japanese companies are stronger in entertainment software or "emotion moving" software. He expects this trend to continue.

The speaker concluded his talk by discussing some emerging new developments which may accelerate the Japanese information revolution by five or ten years:

- *The recent rapid increase in i-Mode mobile telephone service,* which combines digital mobile telephone and Internet service. In the first six months after this service started in April 1999, two million subscribers signed up and 1700 i-Mode websites were established. Some people say that this type of Internet utilization might be mainstream in the future in Japan, edging out the use of the fixed terminal.

- *The new Sony television game machine, Play Station 2,* introduced in September 1999. This machine has a specially designed, powerful CPU inside with four functions: game machine, Internet terminal, DVD player, and CD player. Projected sales in Japan are 20 million units. This would mean 50% family penetration in a few years. Play Station2 might even become the new home terminal that is more than "just" a game machine.

- *The broad-band fiber-optic telecommunication network* that NTT is rushing to construct all over Japan that covers the "last one mile" in urban areas, and the digitized satellite broadcasting systems that will start in a few years. Both of these will enable interactive services at home through the television set. These new systems may be another driver for the Japanese information revolution because, as the speaker indicated earlier, TV penetration in Japanese society is very high.

- *The emergence of new net consumers.* Within a few years all the Japanese primary and secondary schools will be connected to the Internet. Computer and network literacy lectures will be given to children in the school. They will be the future net consumers. Presently, the younger generation, from university students to young businessmen under 35 yeas old, have already had plenty of Internet experience at their offices and homes. Their life style and communication patterns are now changing, through the Internet and the use of mobile communication tools. For many university students, personal computers and the Internet are becoming absolute necessities in their campus lives. Some retired persons more than 60 years old are also becoming new net consumers. They experienced PC and Internet usage at their offices and, after retirement, they continue using the Internet for various purposes.

- *New distribution channels.* A new distribution channel related to the Internet which reflects uniquely Japanese characteristics is the Multi-media KIOSK

Network at convenience stores. In Japanese urban areas, convenience stores like 7-11 are placed in very dense patterns and most of them are open 24 hours per day. They are becoming a necessity for urban consumers. Recently, in relation to Internet shopping, these convenience stores are gathering attention as a means for paying or receiving goods, like books, CDs, or other commodities.

The speaker believes that these are some of the emerging trends that will be characteristic of the Japanese Information Revolution over the next 10 to 20 years. He closed by stating that the speed of change in Japanese society as a whole is generally not fast. However, he expects the areas of technology, business, the market, and consumption to change faster than other areas of human life such as emotion, culture, and social customs.

Bridging the Digital Divide: The Indian Story

The next speaker discussed the course of the information revolution in India. After providing background information on relevant events in India over the period since independence in 1947, he described the current state of the Indian IT industry:

- The Indian IT industry is focused primarily on computer software, and is largely export oriented. In addition to software developers working in India, there is a large Indian diaspora of IT professionals, in the U.S. and elsewhere around the world.

- Today there are some 250,000 software professionals in India. Each year, about 170,000 engineers graduate from Indian universities, many of whom go into the software area.[26]

- There are several hundred software companies operating in India today, with annual revenues totaling over $2.5 billion in 1997-1998. Industry-wide, total revenues have been growing at a rate of about 50% per year over the last few years. Many individual companies have 50-70% annual revenue growth rates. Many of these Indian companies are listing on the NASDAQ over-the-counter stock market.[27]

- New Indian software companies are constantly emerging; recently there have been an average of two initial public offerings (IPOs) every week.

----

[26] India graduates more engineers every year than the U.S.

[27] The speaker described listing on NASDAQ has having replaced attaining "Nirvana" as the life dream of many young Indian professionals.

- In addition to software firms in India itself, Indian professionals are among the most numerous founders of Silicon Valley start-ups in recent years.

- Software companies in India tend to be grouped in geographic clusters. The two largest clusters are around Mumbai (Bombay), with roughly 21% of the firms, and around Bangalore, with about 19% of the firms.

- These Indian software companies are very much "wired in" to the global software market, and diversified across a wide range of software products. Many of them work as software subcontractors and vendors to major North American and European information technology and information/financial services companies (e.g., Microsoft, Citygroup, etc.).

- Successful Indian software firms are all run along "democratic" rather than traditional hierarchical lines. Thus far, no family-owned firms with hierarchical management structures have succeeded in the Indian software industry.

The speaker mentioned two other nations that are emerging as major international software players: Israel and Ireland. Taken together, India, Israel, and Ireland are sometimes referred to as "the three I's" insofar as their software industries are concerned. Table 7.2 compares the software industries in these three nations. Today the Irish software industry is considerably larger than that of India.[28] However, the Indian industry is growing much faster.

Table 7.2

The Three I's: Ireland, India, and Israel

	Total Software Revenues (1997-1998)	Annual Revenue Growth Rates
Ireland	$6.5 billion	14%
India	$2.7 billion	50%
Israel	$1.5 billion	17%

Thus far, the Indian IT industry, for all its vitality, has had a minimal impact on the Indian national economy and society. The roughly 250,000 software professionals working in India represent less than 0.3% of India's population (960 million). The roughly $2.5 billion in annual software revenues represents

---

[28] Indeed, Ireland is the second largest exporter of software products in the world today, after only the U.S.

about 0.6% of India's annual GDP ($414 billion). Thus far, the Indian software industry is a thin veneer of top of the Indian economy and society.

The speaker listed several obstacles that India must overcome to spread the benefits of the information revolution more widely across Indian society:

- *The three C's: connectivity, computers, and contents.* Less than 1% of Indians have access to computers; even fewer are connected to the Internet. Much/most of the content of the World Wide Web today is not relevant to the average Indian.

- *Computers versus jobs.* There is a concern in some Indian circles that computers, viewed as a labor saving device, will eliminate jobs. This mitigates against the introduction of computers into many areas of the Indian economy.

- *The digital divide.* In India, this divide exists not only between rich and poor, but also between north and south. Today, most of the educational institutions training software professionals and other engineers, and most of the clusters of software firms, are in the southern portion of the country. The south is well ahead of the north, insofar as the information age is concerned.

- *Transparency versus controls.* Historically, the Indian economy has been subject to extensive state controls, with little transparency into government decisions affecting the economy. In recent years there has been the beginnings of a move to privatization, freer markets, etc., but India still has a way to go.

- *Human resources.* Insofar as information technology and the information age are concerned, India has vast untapped human resources. Tapping these resources is a major challenge.

As one step towards overcoming these obstacles, India has recently begun the Sankhya Vahini program. Over the next three to five years, this program will:

- Create a high-speed (2.5 Gbps and higher), optical-fiber national Internet backbone for India, extending across the entire country.

- Connect large numbers of Indian towns and provide them access to the national backbone and international gateways.

- Create "metro rings" (i.e., metropolitan area networks) in key cities (six in the first year).

- Provide users (corporations, software companies, ISPs, educational institutions, etc.) high-speed Internet access.

54

- Provide enriched education and entertainment content and other value-added services.

- Create a data network that is commercially viable and amenable to scaling up.

The speaker views this program as a major step towards bringing India more fully into the information age and using IT to improve the lot of the Indian citizenry. As the speaker said regarding India: "We missed out on the industrial revolution. We don't want to miss out on the information revolution."

The Information Revolution at the Margins: E-Economy, E-Security and E-Equity in Africa

The speaker began by noting that throughout the world there is a strong correlation between national income and Internet penetration. Generally speaking, nations with higher GDPs have greater Internet penetration into their societies; nations with lower GDPs, lower Internet penetration. Africa is one of the poorest regions of the world.[29] As such, its nations have (with a few exceptions) among the lowest GDPs in the entire world and, along with this, the lowest penetration of the Internet, other aspects of IT, and the information revolution into their societies and economies.[30]

What IT penetration there is into Africa is very unevenly distributed. For example, of the roughly 3 million computers in Africa today, about half are in South Africa, 1/6 in Nigeria, 1/6 in North Africa, and the other 1/6 scattered across the rest of Africa.

And the "IT" generally available to the average person in Africa is of quite a different mixture that in developed nations. For example, for every telephone line in Africa, there are about 2000 TVs.

The speaker noted that the economic structure of any nation can be divided into three major components: agriculture, manufacturing, and information work. In many/most of the G-7 nations today, information work has become the largest component, with manufacturing smaller, and agriculture smaller still. In Asia and Latin America, speaking broadly, manufacturing is the largest component,

---

[29] As one example of how poor Africa is, relative to the industrialized world, the speaker noted that the wealthiest 15 individuals in the world, taken together, have a greater net worth than all of sub-Saharan Africa.

[30] Today, 99.5% of Africans are not connected to the Internet.

with agriculture smaller, and information work the smallest component, but growing rapidly.

In most of Africa today, in contrast, agriculture is by far the largest component. Manufacturing and information work are both tiny. To a large extent, Africa is still in the agricultural age. Most of Africa, and most Africans, never made it into the industrial age, let alone the information age.

That is today. What about tomorrow? The speaker identified three key things required if Africa is to get into the information age: leadership, vision, and institutional change. Today, these are lacking in many -- but not all -- African nations.

In their reaction to the information revolution, the speaker believes that African nations will fall into three categories:

- *Leaders.* Insofar as sub-Sahara Africa is concerned, South Africa is the only nation in this category today.
- *Adaptors.*
- *Late comers.*

It is too soon to tell which African nations will be Adaptors and which Late Comers. He listed the following structural factors as serving to determine this in each nation, along with the aforementioned leadership and vision factors:

- Employment patterns
- Domestic trade and investment
- Population distribution across regions
- Elite structure and interests
- Political party alignments
- Definition of national interest
- Definition of foreign policy

In closing, the speaker envisaged three possible scenarios for the future course of the information revolution in Africa:

- Africa is most affected by the information revolution of all regions on Earth (e.g., by the use of telemedicine, e-education, etc.). Leapfrogging occurs.
- Africa becomes even further marginalized. There is a continuing lack of communication services and reliable institutions. No leapfrogging occurs.

- Africa becomes even more internally heterogeneous. Some governments seize the initiative; others don't.

8.   North, Central, and South America

Discussion Leader: C. Richard Neu
Rapporteur: Martin Libicki

Approach

This breakout group was tasked to look at the impact of information technology on both North and South America. Roughly speaking, it spent 70 percent of the time on the United States, 5 percent of the time on Canada, and the rest on Latin America.

The United States

Three broad but interrelated areas attracted the bulk of the discussion: the future ubiquity of the Internet, the impact of information technologies on societal disparities, and the potentially disruptive consequences of e-commerce.

The Future Ubiquity of the Internet

How deeply will the Internet penetrate? Will it be a plaything of the top 60 percent of the population (as cable is today) or will it be as ubiquitous as over-the-air broadcast television? Economics drove the group to a mixed answer. Low-bandwidth over-the-phone services that required no more than a fancy handset to acquire would be universal. The higher-bandwidth entertainment-level services that would likely be billed separately would have statistics similar to cable in 2020; it might be considered near-universal at perhaps the 70 to 80 percent level. That said, some urban poor would sooner buy cable than telephone service.

The group consensus saw the Internet of 2020 as driven by entertainment (more than half of all Internet bits today are streaming media: telephony, audio, video) and not necessarily news, shopping, or knowledge in general. Left unknown was whether the services that piggyback on entertainment -- e.g., e-commerce, or even browsing -- will be used by those who bought into the Internet for other reasons. Feelings seemed to be that, by 2020, what is exciting and still being discovered today will be considered utilitarian tomorrow, with people having long ago made up their minds on whether to enjoy this or that service. Left to be determined is whether the Next Generation Internet project will develop Internet uses not yet anticipated today.

Will some technologies be stopped? Despite possible concerns over privacy (and thus some requirement to protect data), there was no indication that information technology would be slowed down any. What public backlash may ensue is likely to be small-scale and disassociated and have little ultimate effect. There are few levers for halting those technologies that no longer depended on government support or even much government approval. Biotechnology is another story, with existing limitations already on genetic research in Europe and research using stem cells and fetal tissue in the United States.

Potential Impacts on the Construct of Society

The disenfranchisement of the information-poor will continue and likely exacerbate.[31] This, despite the probable emergence of easy-to-use applications that require less sophistication to get something useful from it. Five years ago, for instance, one had to fly frequently to understand how to garner the best airfares; today, priceline.com substitutes for sophistication.

Will the public information spaces today erode in the face of small exclusive groups? Tomorrow, so-called "inside/insight clusters" may resemble today's The Well: a 5000-person by-invitation-only group founded by Stewart Brand and originally limited to Northern California. Select people in such clusters would trade inside information and insights to each other without letting the greater public into their discussion.

The decline of democratizing institutions led to the question: whither trade unions? Even though unions are fading in importance, the inequality that unions were established to mitigate is increasing: does this suggest a role for some substitute institution? And if so, what kind? No one in the group could come up with any substitutes that were credible.

----

[31] For instance, the common practice of UPS to drop expensive packages on suburban doorsteps without getting a signature would not work in the inner city; thus e-commerce becomes more expensive there.

How will the virtualization of commerce also affect other critical values such as governance or culture? No one expected the Government to be an important factor in technological development anymore; it is, at best, irrelevant, and, at worst, a nuisance. But if governance erodes, who will be doing the regulation? Can industry be counted on to self-regulate in ways that are considered legitimate by the public? Again, the group could more clearly see institutions in sunset than assess the character of those whose sun might be rising. So, it was feared that although the public would be deeply skeptical of self-regulation, it would also be skeptical of external regulation (a response that echoes the polling data on the Microsoft antitrust case).

As a general rule, the prior totems of national cultures seem to be eroding as well, and today's fads are increasingly global in character. According to one study, only 48 hours are required for a fad to spread around the world in the population of hip 12 to 14 year olds. One result may be that while we do not share the same education (e.g., Milton) we do share the same corporate-derived cultural icons. But this is culture at the superficial level. In the main, information technology enhances factionalism. For instance, the one oddball in each town with an esoteric interest (e.g., old reruns of "Car 54, Where are You") can find similar oddballs in other towns; hitherto, each was isolated.

Much of the discussion also returned to the impact of information technology on privacy and security. A salient issue may be the deliberate use of personal information. There is a sea-change underway not only in the amount of information collected on individual consumers, but also in the degree which such information can be exploited, and the values to which the market is putting on such data for the purposes of micro-marketing. Indeed, efficiencies in exploiting personal data will become a major battleground for corporate preeminence. This leads to a paradox: we want personal service (that is, we want those who would sell us goods and services to know what we want), but we feel less comfortable about the giving up of privacy that goes along with being more well known. And it will become increasingly hard to opt out of a system that traces one's every financial move.

Many forces other than e-commerce are turning the United States into a glass-walled society. Cell phones will routinely have GPS devices built into them. (Current technology already allows them to indicate which cell they are closest to.) Four to five million surveillance cameras are already at work in the United States, with public places accounting for an increasing percentage of them. The marriage of IT (in the form of smaller and more powerful sensors) and biotechnology may result in the wiring to the Internet of those under institutional or medical watch. For instance, someone who earlier would have been incarcerated for having committed a crime would, instead, be wired so that increased hormone levels associated with impending violence would precipitate a warning to headquarters coupled with the release of a calming agent into the bloodstream. Will sensors be something that only the powerful control? The most likely answer was that sensors would be controlled by those who had interests that sensor information would serve, and that, yes, they would tend to be (but would not have to be) the powerful.

Worse may be the possibility that surveillance and classification technologies that are used more-or-less benignly in the United States, may be used in less friendly fashions when sold to third world governments. In the meantime, the longer the U.S. environment remains benign, the longer surveillance technologies will be allowed to advance without being stopped by public opposition.

Another threat may come from criminals who use computer hacking to steal data from original collectors. The former may be fastidious about its use; the recipients of purloined data, meanwhile, are less likely to be bound by such restrictions. In the meantime, consumer resistance to sending one's credit card number through the ether is rapidly fading, and so one potential barrier to e-commerce in its present form is coming down. Although the financial industry is confident that it can reduce unintended leaks of information, someone who ran big networks muttered darkly that there was a lot that a hacker could do to them. Their security problems are worse than DoD's because they invite the potential adversary into the system -- only they are called customers.

Security policy is intimately connected with customer trust and how much one empowers the customer. The answer is not to cut off all the links but to find ways of exercising damage control. Risk control has to become an important and everyday aspect of doing business -- and risk profiles change every quarter. Overall, "back ends" (that part of a computer system that does the internal processing rather than interacting directly with the consumer) are hard to protect. Only time will tell whether bad guys or good guys pull ahead. In the last three years at least, functionality has been purchased at the expense of security. Business people, themselves, have to be able to know whether they have been attacked by individuals or nation-states (and if the latter, then all bets are off and corporations are likely to call on their government to help them).

Side-Effects of E-commerce

Another question was how far e-commerce would transform the U.S. landscape (almost literally). Business-to-business transactions are already squeezing out the ranks of purchasing managers. *Webvan* estimates that every warehouse it establishes eliminates 30 supermarkets -- and their goods turn over far faster, leaving a net reduction in floor space. Banks, for instance, have 6000 acres under roof nationwide -- who will need that kind of space in a future in which people need no longer appear in public areas to acquire goods? So the question recurred: what communities are likely to be hollowed out as the e-commerce wave rolls on? One answer might be: fewer than expected because most commercial jobs are spread more-or-less evenly in proportion to the number of consumers in an area. Instead, the hollowing-out would be everywhere, but more likely to be noticed in slow-growing areas while fast-growing areas quickly filled in the surplus floor space with new activities.

Where might virtual clustering replace physical clustering (e.g., Silicon Valley) -- or will physical contact retain its importance (especially in cultures where face-to-face contact is still key to managing the trust relationship)? The tendency was to believe that face-to-face still mattered. Yet, face-to-face needs would more likely spur get-togethers for meetings rather than the concentrating of workers for getting routine jobs done. One consequence of widespread e-commerce may be a shift away from sales and/or value-added taxes and towards income taxes as a funding source for the government -- posing particular problems for regions (e.g., Latin America) where such taxes are hard to collect.

Techniques of consumer manipulation are growing more sophisticated. Supporting technologies include data mining, a better understanding of how adaptive agents work, and even knowledge of how the human brain works. Thus, the best producers speak of putting consumers on a "journey" that lets them off at a decision to buy a product. But NGOs are also proving adept at pointing out what they call the "con job" that consumers are subject to. Take the controversy over genetically manipulated foods that started in Europe and then migrated, in part, to the United States. Although the reactions of farmers and consumers were intensively modeled by adaptive agent techniques, NGOs started talking about "demon seeds," a potent psychological talisman. So even Archer-Daniels Midland, a giant U.S.-based food processing company, is segregating genetically modified from "natural" farm products. Even in the regulatorily benign United States, some forms of product-based coercion may arise: notably anti-smoking pressures.

Increasingly, the rest of the world is beginning to regard the United States as a big and not necessarily welcome data sink. Europeans, for instance, are very upset about the newly-discovered capability of the NSA (working in concert with its counterparts in other English-speaking countries) to intercept anyone's telephone conversations and fax transmittals. (Whether they have the trained manpower to actually listen to what they intercept remains a different issue.)

Perhaps more controversial is the way that the United States is being increasingly used as a data center in ways that may violate privacy norms overseas. Europeans (and Canadians) feel that corporations are using global networking to get around EU (or Canadian) rules regarding what information may be collected and for what purposes. The U.S. tendency is to leave privacy issues to voluntary self-regulation, counting on honest disclosure and the (residual) ability of individuals to withhold private data and walk away from transactions that require it.

Over the next twenty years, the privacy violations that gain attention may come less from curious governments than from quasi-legitimate businesses who can exploit personal information for blackmail and coercion. Meanwhile, everyone would have to put up with everyday violations as anonymous others know and exploit for marketing purposes personal features that not everyone is comfortable revealing to the world.

But the government will not be entirely innocent. Surveillance technology may be used to facilitate the work of agencies such as the Immigration and Naturalization Service -- raising, again, the issue of a national identity card (even as the credit card itself moves closer to becoming a private national identity card). The dispossessed may come to be known as the "sin tarjetas" (without cards).

Latin America

Although the penetration of the Internet into Latin America is likely to run at least ten years behind the United States (and some rural areas are unlikely to see much service at all unless cellular telephony becomes very inexpensive), many of the same issues -- such as disenfranchisement -- are likely to become, if anything, even more salient. Indigenous people, for instance, have almost no hope of being IT participants. The privileged, largely urban classes are likely to move closer to the United States. Thus new cleavages may form and old ones cut deeper.

The initial question addressed by the group was what contribution information technology would play in the development of Latin America. Answers were mixed. Countries such as the Dominican Republic had deep-seated woes that IT was unlikely to do much for. Other countries, such as Costa Rica, had inherent advantages and would be able to participate much more widely. Countries that have the Internet connectivity and can therefore better host retired and quasi-retired Americans will benefit.

Which is not to say that Latin America is ignorant of IT. Allende, in the early 1970s, started to implement a cybernetic centralized control planning system for the Chilean economy -- then the Chicago free-market model took over. Today Chile is using auctions to bring about universal telephone service; this is having the ironic result that Chileans may rise in revolt against companies such as Bell Atlantic. Narcoterrorists are very savvy in leveraging technology. Dollarization is also proceeding apace. By 2020, Latin America is likely to have open telecommunications markets.

Overall, the region is likely to be disadvantaged in IT (relative to the West or East Asia); they'll be takers not makers.

First, Latin America has no regional organizations. Indeed, the continent has very little interior with almost every country oriented towards their coastline, and having better communication pipelines to the West (i.e., North America and Western Europe) than they have with each other.[32]

Second, Latin America has no lead country doing anything really innovative. Chile might be were its sudden ascent to riches not feeding regional resentment.

Third, Latin America enjoys an awkward and dominating relationship with the United States.

Fourth, Latin America still has a last mile problem, especially outside the urban areas (again, wireless may provide the silver bullet). Overall, integration into the world economy will remain problematic.

Still, the common language (except for Brazil) and culture of the area may lead to a regional identity proportional to and prompted by the fact that everyone can access the same media (and on-line communities) at the same time. Conversely, there is increasing likelihood that the United States will be intertwined with Latin American problems for demographic if not other reasons.

In briefing the results of the group discussion to the entire conference audience, several respondents in the larger audience took issue with the supposition that Latin America was especially hostile to technology, afflicted with sharp divisions, or even particularly backwards. One offered the opinion that Latin America was certainly further ahead than Africa, the Middle East, and South Asia. Another observed that the ABC countries (i.e., Argentina, Brazil, and

----

[32] This phenomenon is broader than just Latin American. Two random countries anywhere in the world are likely to switch their packets to each other in the United States -- a state of affairs resented in Europe and Japan and one which is bound to undergo change.

Chile) had achieved an urban civilization that would not be out of place on the European side of the Mediterranean.

Canada

A brief discussion of Canada raised the question of what aspects of Canada's social model can be preserved in the onrush to globalization. As barriers around the world go down, the top-level logic by which Canada's institutions deal with the outside world would have to conform. This would limit the scope of independence (or Government social regulation), but it was unclear how that would affect the relationship between institutions and the Canadian consumer (e.g., in health care, or community banking).

The consensus seemed to be that Canada would try to preserve its culture. Yet, it was not clear how it would do that when restrictions on broadcasting, mail deliveries, or book sales that apply to physical space cannot be applied in cyberspace. Indeed as the scope for serious social governance differences with the United States narrowed, cultural distinctions (often token ones) would be created in its stead.

9. Europe

Discussion Leader: Ian Pearson
Rapporteur: Tora Bikson

Approach

This group began with an open brainstorming session intended to identify major political, economic and social issues raised by the information revolution that had not, in the view of participants, been sufficiently addressed in the conference plenary sessions. Such issues would be of concern to Europe but not exclusively so. Next the group focused its attention on information revolution questions and projections that are either unique to or particularly characteristic of Europe. It subsequently addressed various kinds of modifying factors that would affect the pace and shape of the information society in different parts of Europe. Finally, the group reviewed the range of ideas it had generated and attempted to capture them in four possible future scenarios for Europe. The discussion that follows is ordered to reflect the organization of the group process summarized here.

General Issues for the Future of the Information Revolution

Other Revolutions

Continuing advances in computing and communications technology have stimulated an information revolution that will fuel revolutions in a number of other domains such as science, engineering, health/medicine, business, manufacturing, the environment, transportation and lifestyle. A valuable future task, therefore, would be to identify those domains where positive feedback loops will likely occur (such as the expected synergy between biological science and IT) and then devise policies to guide the impact for greatest societal benefit.

Social Consequences

Greater consideration should be given to the future social consequences of the information revolution. For example, it is likely that further automation as a function of technological advance will create more jobs than it eliminates. However, attending just to net gains ignores the social disruption that may occur (since job losers and job gainers may well not be the same individuals) as well as the need imposed on all workers for continuous learning and the social stress of unending change. (Stress reduction will likely become a major concern in countries proceeding rapidly through the information revolution.)

Demographic dimensions of countries moving ahead in the information revolution also merit consideration. While noting that demography is not destiny, group members believe that the aging population of most industrial nations suggests that a great deal of work will be outsourced over networks to developing countries in the future, terming this trend "virtual migration." On the other hand, older people may be mobilized by such technology both politically and socially--since participation will demand less in the way of physical mobility. In any case, an older population of IT users should be expected to seek a new range of support services (including not only technical support but also health and social services) that could be either delivered or enhanced by digital networks.

Other social consequences noted in the breakout group include the ways in which physical or geographic proximity are implicated in creativity and innovation; there is a need to illuminate these processes and to understand the limits of IT-based connectivity in supporting them. On the other hand, increased geographic mobility together with far-ranging connectivity are likely to bring about transnational--and even global--virtual communities of varied kinds. Finally, the group underscored its concern about the future concentration of social elites, attributable to the differential benefits they will accrue from the information revolution.

Information-Intensive Goods and Services

The conference plenary sessions gave significant attention to technology and connectivity. Future study should pay more attention to the content and uses of information-intensive goods and services.

Presently such goods and services are consumed mainly by businesses. While households and individuals increasingly confront IT-embedded objects (cars, coffee-makers and a range of other goods were offered in evidence), these do not directly require the consumer to interact with considerable amounts of information per se. Information-intensive goods and services, on the other hand, remain a small fraction of the consumption function (compared, for example, with housing, food, transportation and the like). Further, they require substantial amounts of time and effort to be consumed; their consumption is therefore probably self-limiting. Projecting the potential market would be an enlightening exercise--today's estimates may be overrated.

Could technical barriers be overcome, the group identified two significant categories of information-intensive goods and services that should have dramatic value for the future of the global information revolution. The first is educational technology, including both a very low cost access device and appropriately delivered education and training content. When available, such technology will help enable even those with least education all over the world to participate in the information society. The second is language translation technology, again including both a low-cost device with adequate power and speed to make real-time translation viable and sufficiently intelligent software to make it useful. The group urged pushing for both these potential breakthroughs.

System Governance

As society becomes increasingly dependent on internetworking to conduct a vast range of political, social and economic activities, the risks posed by potential instability and disruption (whether intentional or inadvertent) become great. Major chaos, for example, could ruin even large banks. System vulnerability should therefore be probed in future work.

Further, agreements about rights and norms will have to be established across national boundaries. For example, nations will have to come to agreements about protection of privacy versus the near-limitless possibilities for surveillance of network-based activity. The pervasiveness of surveillance, for instance, could become a flashpoint between the European Union (EU) and the US regarding privacy.

This area of contention is just one of many future domains where system governance issues will have to be decided and overarching agreements will have to be reached. Governments will have to negotiate with one another, suggesting the need for some sort of overriding transnational vehicle (much like the EU now provides for European nations). However, it is unclear how any such agreements, however brokered, would be enforced.

Prospects and Problems for Europe in the Information Revolution

The European Context

Europe comprises an extremely dense and complex group of independent nations that embody many different languages, cultures and constitutions. It has a long history that may also be a source of inertia. But its great diversity should be a source of strength, providing an incredibly varied pool from which social forms highly suited for survival in the information society of the future may emerge, adapt and grow.

Currently European nations are trying to add a layer of federation (via the EU). Currently--the EU parliament and commission notwithstanding—the power is still mainly in the national states; and there is considerable debate over how much power to hand over to EU bodies. Nonetheless, citizens are increasingly independent of their national states and some degree of political integration is already apparent. These trends support and are supported by the information revolution. It is likely that the near term will bring even greater regional integration across national boundaries (e.g., in the Baltics and in the Mediterranean region). Such prospects are shored up by long historical ties, shared social networks and cultural preferences--all of which are frequently grounded in locality. The group also noted the importance of tacit understanding, which often plays a role in political, economic and social trust.

IT in Europe

The Internet is still at an early stage ("ebay and amazon.com are industrial age organizations on a modern platform"). Europe missed the first phase of the Internet, and so has spent much of the past decade or so playing catch-up. Further, Europe has an old legacy infrastructure--there is no fast broadband network linking major European cities. These factors may slow the pace of the information revolution there.

On the other hand, Europe could emerge as a front runner in the next phase, for several reasons. First, Europe has traditionally been strong in telecommunications and broadcasting, and has led the way in cellular technology. Second--and related--is the point that Europe has a reasonable approach to technology standards, arriving at constructive solutions that facilitate interoperability without precluding innovation. Third, there are immediate incentives (given the density of cultures and multiplicity of languages noted above) to achieve voice recognition and real-time translation; these should stimulate related technical advances. Moreover, Europe should continue to be a leader in the production of content, and could also be a leader in breakthrough uses of IT. Finally, several European countries are outpacing the US in R&D investment; such investment may be viewed as a forerunner of technological innovation.

Expectations: Governments, Markets and Technologies

Europe has far less confidence than the US in the ability of "free" markets to lead to productive and healthy information societies. There are doubts about whether the same style of capitalism that promoted a competitive industrial economy will work equally well in the post-industrial age; and there is skepticism about whether the information revolution in the US is really being driven by a free market in the first place (versus, for example, Microsoft and the Federal Reserve).

In Europe, therefore, governments are more likely to intervene in the course of the information revolution so that its shape there will likely differ from what emerges in the US. First, governments in Europe will likely attempt to intervene in the market in a balanced way to span the digital divide, promote equity, protect privacy and assure inclusion and social participation (or reduce marginalization). At the same time, European governments will give greater emphasis to social and cultural capital development and to the quality of life in the information society. Further, in Europe unions also exert an influence, limiting the power of governments and the market in the service of the quality of working life. So Europe may provide lifestyle models for the future (in contrast to the US, where the market will be allowed to determine the landscape of the information society).

Expectations: Business Environment

The nature of government intervention in the business environment will be a key factor in shaping the information society in Europe. In general, the trend will be to let industries self-organize and self-regulate, but to introduce government intervention to keep competition fair and to avoid misbehavior on the part of players in the market.

Europe, like other parts of the industrial world, has witnessed the IT-enabled implementation of lean organizations and the intensification of work all the way up and down the hierarchy of firms. But it has been slower at restructuring than the US, in part because of the serious social disruption and personal stress brought about by these changes. Europe has also been slower to engender new high-technology start-up firms. It is likely that these tendencies won't change. So Europe should undergo evolutionary change in the business world, in which old "dinosaur" companies that can't adapt go extinct while new or more agile old firms survive.

Work intensification in restructured firms is associated both with higher stress and longer working hours. These outcomes run counter to the European emphasis on quality of life in general and, in particular, on shorter working hours than most of the industrialized world. To retain these values, Europe will have to deploy advancing IT in ways that make productivity break-throughs if its firms are to retain competitive advantage in the global economy while its people adhere to shorter working weeks and longer vacations.

Meanwhile, unions are concerned about how best to organize and maintain their voice when, as a function of the information revolution in business, people work in so many places (at the workplace, to be sure, but also at home, in hotels, in transit, at client firms, and so on). It is unclear who will assure workplace health and safety, equitable processes and rewards, and so on in the future. More generally, traditional trade or industry unions don't cope well with evolution and change. It would not be surprising, therefore, to see the rise of professional guilds in Europe--new kinds of organizations (not entirely unlike the old guilds) that will promote firm self-regulation and provide guides for positive working conditions in IT-enabled enterprises. Such guilds might be transnational, just as firms are.

At the same time, the new e-commerce business environment should empower individual consumers and groups of consumers. Specifically, by bundling products and services in distinctive ways, firms can produce "tailored" or customized outputs that meet an individual's needs and preferences. Individuals can readily shop around for the items they want, comparing prices online to arrive at the best buy. Finally, ease of network-based coordination should enable collective buying, where organized consumer groups can bargain with sellers for large-scale purchases at reduced cost.

Expectations: Education and the Transformation of Information into Knowledge

The European educational tradition is very old and very strong, and this strength should continue into the future. It provides the foundation for developing knowledge from information and leads to an emphasis on information quality (versus information per se). These are especially important given the incredible pace of knowledge growth, the sheer difficulty of keeping up, and the increasingly overwhelming difficulty of filtering.

Europe's traditional strengths in education and the transformation of information into knowledge, coupled with its edge in broadcasting (see above) should thus make it a content leader in the future in remote education, news and varied lifestyle arenas. Additionally, if it can transform content into "brands," it may well be able to generate significant revenue streams from its content advantage.

Other Expectations: Groups and Leaders

Like the rest of the world, Europe expects to see the rise of virtual communities of all kinds, including social groups, collegial networks and even virtual families. In particular, participants foresaw these developments occurring much more rapidly among younger individuals, who already share a "youth culture" that transcends national boundaries. It is possible, then, that generational divisions may mark the information society of the near future.

Besides groups, participants raised questions about future intellectual and political leadership (since visionary leaders can by themselves exert a profound societal influence). Where, for instance, will the next daVinci come from? Or the next Marx? Or the next labor organizer who can unite the growing cadre of IT workers of the world? Many believed that Europe might well be their origin.

Modifying Factors

In general, breakout group participants viewed the North-South split (in Europe) as representative of a cluster of modifying factors that would differentially shape the course of the information revolution there. At present, the split marks a digital divide, with IT penetration and connectivity much greater in the North. The North also typically experiences a more rapid rate of diffusion of new technologies, so the divide is likely to widen. Moreover, although southern and northern countries are both committed to norms of social equity, governments in the South will not take a proactive stance toward the introduction and promotion of IT (in contrast to the agendas of northern governments).

Along East-West lines, participants noted that most of eastern Europe is eager to join the EU and other West-dominated alliances. While the East generally lags the West in IT penetration and connectivity, it has the advantage of a strong educational tradition (in mathematics and the sciences as well as literacy). Thus eastern Europe, and especially Russia, should be able to move forward faster than many countries at a similar stage of penetration and connectivity. Long-standing historic and cultural relationships should play a substantial role in shaping the emergence of network alliances in Europe.

Besides these general themes, participants generated examples of other more specific modifying factors (while cautioning that these should be regarded as illustrative but not exhaustive). In the Nordic countries, for instance, there is a strong emphasis on rapid but equal diffusion of IT to retain the current socioeconomic structure (in which status divisions are small). There is also a strong commitment to consensual decision making, which may slow the pace of change. Finally, Nordic citizens place a high value on home life, so it would be natural to see there the emergence of IT-at-home applications.

Eastern Europe on the whole, and Russia in particular, has increasing opportunities for closer integration with the West in the information society of the future. High education levels plus relatively low labor costs should give it a special competitive niche in IT (potentially very strong in software and in content production). Currently, however, trust in banks is very low and there is little to no protection for intellectual property rights. These trends, together with the existence of large black and gray markets, mean that e-commerce is not presently viable. That situation could change rapidly with economic and political stability. (The remarkable success of Estonia would be worth special examination in this context.)

In western Europe, meanwhile, France has less confidence in IT as a social good and more skepticism about the economics of large-scale network-based coordination. The UK views itself as attempting to conserve its traditional cultural strengths, values and language, proceeding with a balanced and constructive approach to the information revolution. But it was acknowledged that "not everyone in Europe thinks exactly as the Brits do" about preserving the past.

Possible Future Scenarios

To arrive at possible futures, breakout group participants started by insisting that the picture will not be generated by looking simply at IT. Rather, participants suggested envisioning an n-dimensional space within which individuals and groups engage in numerous and diverse interactions along political, institutional, educational, economic, social, personal and other as yet unforeseen lines. Then they sought to discern the conditions that could cause these interactions to

73

cluster, yielding distinctly different scenarios. Figure 9.1 below summarizes the results of that exercise.

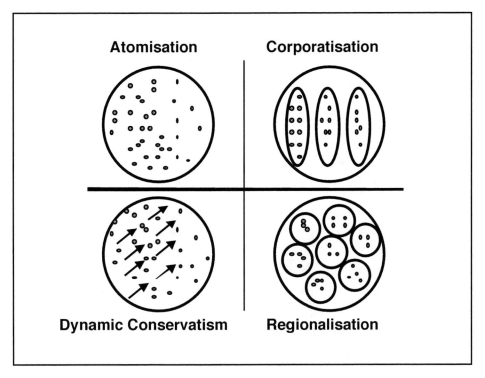

Figure 9.1 Four Future Scenarios for Europe

The upper left quadrant reflects organic atomisation, presenting a biomimetic model of the European information society of the future. This model incorporates thousands and thousands of small units engaging in millions of interactions that are organically self-organizing and self-adapting. It recalls complexity theory, as used to comprehend the voluminous and ever-changing constellations of transactions hosted and monitored by Citibank; it also rests on the future vision of network-based auctions, markets, reconfigurable work teams and "e-lance" labor that characterizes recent organizational behavior research. Finally, the picture is consistent with the view that highly complex information societies -- like large complex information systems -- cannot be both designed and robust; hence they must rely on a more organic, or biomimetic, approach to development and sustainability.

The upper right quadrant, labeled corporatisation, portrays a quite different future, In this scenario, a small number of very large players negotiate with one another to exert social, economic and other control over individual-level interactions. These dominating entities may include large transnational enterprises and transnational unions or professional guilds as well as intergovernmental bodies or NGOs. Such a model for Europe reflects the magnifying power of IT (the rich get richer, the big get bigger) along with its capability to support mass coordinated action.

Intense regionalisation is depicted in the lower right quadrant. Here, too, interactions span national boundaries. But they are shaped by cultural, linguistic and historic ties, shared values, and common tacit knowledge about how decisions are made or negotiations undertaken. On this view, for instance, parts of Russia would likely be closely integrated with the Baltic nations, while other parts of Russia might well be integrated into an Asian cluster. The North-South split would probably define some regions as well, with southern Italy part of a Mediterranean cluster and northern Italy linked to other parts of the North.

In the lower left quadrant, dynamic conservatism represents a scenario in which the traditional national governments of Europe come together (for instance, under the EU rubric) to try to preserve what they value most about contemporary society while moving toward the future. They attempt to arrive at shared frameworks for regulation that make room for innovation while establishing a fair playing field for competition. They rely on constructive consensual standards to guide IT development and implementation.

Breakout group participants believe that Europe will start in this last quadrant and try to stay there. But it represents a long, slow, deliberative process. It is therefore susceptible to being overtaken or derailed by other events. For example, a major economic crisis in Europe that requires fast agile responses could put an end to the slow progressive scenario. On the other hand, the legacy infrastructure in Europe could impede its forward movement so that the future information revolution in Europe ends up being led from without.

10. The Asia Pacific Region

Discussion Leader: James Mulvenon
Rapporteur: James Dewar

A Framework

The Asia Pacific group decided early on that some careful definitions were important to the discussion of the impact of the Information Revolution in the Asia Pacific region. Those discussions produced relationships among three concepts -- *technology, artifact* and *usage* -- as shown in Figure 10.1:

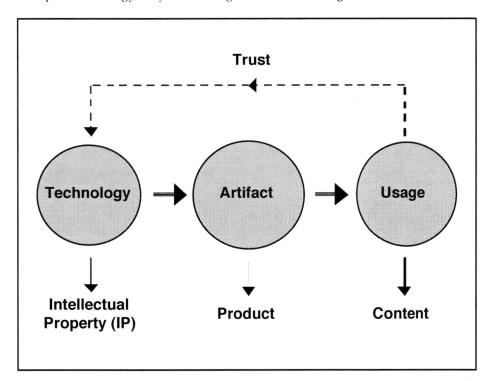

Figure 10.1 Technology, Artifact, and Usage

Technology, here, refers to the idea or intellectual property behind the *artifact* or *product* that embodies it. The distinction here is between countries that have the intellectual capital to create products and countries that are primarily factories or producers of products that were developed elsewhere.

In the simplest terms, the *usage* or *content* concept refers primarily to the consumer market for the technologies and artifacts developed. In this regard, the term "usage" is being used literally to refer to consumers using the products and technologies. Usage engenders "content" because that is often developed locally in each consumer market to suit the tastes or habits of the local market.[33] So content varies and depends on the usage or marketplace. That this item (Usage) requires "trust" simply means that people trust that the gadgets they are relying increasingly on function correctly, will continue to do so, and will remain available.

The group talked about where countries in the region are now and what "branch points" may lead them to become significantly different in the future. It was clear from the discussion that branch points may be very different for different countries in the region.

Asia Pacific Defining Characteristics

Before working on sub-regional aspects of the Information Revolution, the group worked to characterize the Asia Pacific region as a whole in terms of the driving and stunting factors. That led to Table 10.1:

----

[33] For example, the IBM PC is an artifact which is shipped globally. However, the content or software loaded onto it varies depending on to whom the PC is being shipped.

Table 10.1

Driving and Stunting Factors

	Technology (Intellectual Property)	Artifact (Product)	Usage (Content)
Driving Factors	• Education • Equity capital access • Venture spirit • Local market potential	• Tax policy • Plentiful, low-cost labor • "ISP" effect	• Consumer wealth • Taxation policy • "ISP" effect • Quality and availability of service
Stunting Factors	• Over regulation • Government policy • Intellectual property right violations • Monopolies	• Low mfg./process technology • Distribution and sourcing • Legacy systems	• Censorship • Lack of credit • Trust of product • Language

Since almost any entry in the table can be either a driving or a stunting factor the table should be read as follows: Countries/areas with high education, good access to equity capital, a venture spirit and good local market potential are good candidates to become technology providers AND in the Asia Pacific in general, these conditions hold. Similarly, over regulation, disadvantageous government policies, poor handling of intellectual property rights violations and disruptive monopolies will all work to stunt a country/area from becoming a technology provider AND these are certainly in evidence in the Asia Pacific region. How those factors play out in an individual country/area was left until later in the discussion.

Most of the remaining table entries are self explanatory with the exception of the "ISP" effect. This is the ability of an individual or small group to have a quick, disproportionately large effect (as in the early Internet Service Providers). The language stunting factor under *usage* worried about too much of the Information Revolution content being in English for the Asia Pacific region to take quick or easy advantage.

Given the above table, the group further generalized four defining characteristics of the Asia Pacific region with the respect to the Information Revolution:

- Asia Pacific governments actively try to engineer Information Revolution outcomes/directions (and most will be unsuccessful)

- Asia Pacific suffers from a net brain drain in the technology arena (and this is likely to continue)

- Usage in the region will go up significantly

- The Asia Pacific region will be a net software consumer and a net hardware producer for the foreseeable future

Country-by-Country Assessment

The group then turned to sub-regional assessments by country or area. This led to Table 10.2:

There's a good deal of information in the table. We will walk through the entries in the order in which they were discussed. The first point of discussion was the manner in which the region should be broken up. The areas shown in the table were ultimately decided on as being most similar (if grouped) and likely to be or behave differently from other areas.

Chronologically, the next topic of discussion was where each of the areas in the table were today regarding each of the three framework topics (i.e., technology, artifact, and usage). A judgement was made here assigning *high, medium,* or *low* values to each of these topics for each of the areas. For example, Korea was judged to be *low* in technology and *high* in artifact because it is a leading manufacturer and exporter of artifacts, but does not develop the underlying technologies for those products and is not a product innovator. Korea was judged to be *medium* in its use of information technology and products. Similar judgements were made for the other areas shown in the table. The group then adjusted the ratings to give Taiwan a *medium-plus* in technology and a *medium-minus* in usage and to give Oceana a *medium-plus* in usage.

Table 10.2

Country-by-Country Assessment

	Predictability[34]	Technology (IP)	Artifact (Product)	Usage (Content)
Japan	P	High ←→	High ↘	Medium ↑
Korea	MP	Low	High	Medium
China	P	Low ←→	High ↑	Low ↑
Hong Kong	P	Low ←→	Low ↓	High ←→
Taiwan	MP	Medium +	High	Medium −
Singapore/ Malaysia	P	Low ←→	Medium ←→	Medium ↑
SE Asia	UP	Low	Medium	Low
Oceana[35]	P	Medium ↗	Low ↓	Medium + ↑

The group then turned to a discussion of the future and made two judgements. The first judgement was determining how predictable the group thought the various areas were. That is, how reliably did the group think it could project what would happen in each area for each of the three framework topics (technology, artifact, and usage) out to roughly to the year 2020. These judgements are reported in the second column of the table. Surprisingly, the group thought most of the areas were relatively predictable *with respect to the Information Revolution*. No one was willing to predict the geopolitical climate in 2020, but thought that the progress of the Information Revolution would be relatively insensitive to geopolitical and other changes. *The one serious caveat was that there would be no war in the Asia Pacific region in the coming 20 years*. If there were a war, all bets would be off.[36] Only Korea (medium predictable), Taiwan (medium predictable), and SE Asia (unpredictable) came out other than predictable.

The second judgement regarding the future then looked at those areas that were considered predictable and predicted in what direction the group thought an area would go with respect to each of the three factors over the next 20 years. In the above table, ↑ means the group definitely thought that there would be an increase in that

----

[34] P = Predictable, MP = Medium Predictable, UP = Unpredictable.

[35] Including Australia and New Zealand.

[36] In this case, the group decided it should be reconvened to project the future again!

factor in that area. In China, for example, which the group judged to be high already in artifact production, the consensus was that China would be even more of a factor in artifact production in the future. A ↗ means the group thought there would be some movement, ←→ means the area will remain at its current level, ↘ means a slight decrease and ↓ means the group thought there would definitely be a decrease in that factor for that area. In Hong Kong, for example, the group thought there would be even less artifact production in the future.

Technologies That Could Make a Difference

The final action of the group was to identify technologies that they thought would make a big difference in the Asia Pacific region. Six such technologies were identified:

- Non-electric-based computing (or room temperature superconducting). The idea here was that much of the Asia Pacific region has rudimentary or no electricity (and that this is a significant constraint to computer use), so computing that depended very little on electricity could make a big difference.

- Machine translation (or non-von Neuman machines). Because of the many languages in the area and the predominance of English on the Internet, machine translation (or non-von Neuman machines that would allow brute force solutions to machine translation) could drive usage.

- LEO (Low Earth Orbit) ubiquity. These would be satellites that would allow full global coverage at all times. Similar to the first technology, this would allow Internet usage to remote locations.

- PKI (Public Key Infrastructure) for privacy/security and cheap crypto protection. Here the group thought that people in the Asia Pacific region are particularly worried about privacy. More robust security measures may remove significant cultural barriers to Internet usage.

- Digital epidemiology. This is the area that seemed most interesting on the biocomputing front for the Asia Pacific region. Because of the population densities, a wide set of sensors could detect illness outbreaks quickly, then molecular engineering/breeding techniques could be used to create tailored remedies rapidly.

- Non-silicon-based chips. It was thought that this might facilitate fabrication technologies in this artifact production-rich area of the world.

11. Middle East, Africa, and South Asia

Discussion Leader: Ernest Wilson
Rapporteur: Robert Anderson

This breakout group was confronted with a challenging and diverse set of world regions and cultures. Our assignment comprised countries in:

- *Africa*: There are considerable distinctions to be made between South Africa and the remainder of sub-Saharan Africa;

- *The Middle East and North Africa (MENA)*: The predominantly Islamic cultures of the Gulf Arab countries plus Iran, and the countries of North Africa. Included in this region is the more industrialized country of Israel;

- *South Asia*: The predominant countries (in terms of population) are India and Pakistan, but this region also includes Sri Lanka, Bangladesh, Bhutan and Nepal.

The general regional characteristics of these countries – making very general characterizations, for which significant exceptions exist – are that they contain a large fraction of the world's population; their institutions (especially governmental and commercial) are often weak, putting a big premium on individual leadership to make up for deficiencies in institutional strengths; and there exists a problematic nature to a number of societal values (e.g., relating to cooperation among – and recognition of the rights of – ethnic or religious minorities).

General Observations

We began by listing a set of general observations related to information and communication technology (ICT) that distinguish this region from others:

- *Absorptive capacity*. Factors such as price, technological complexity, and dependency on reliable infrastructure services are especially important in determining the region's ability to absorb new ICT artifacts and services.

82

Any one of the above factors, among others, may preclude the ability of countries and cultures within the region to adopt and spread an ICT technology to the point where it makes a real difference in the lives of ordinary citizens.

- *Defining "access."* Too often, there is casual talk of a region's "access" to technology, when it is merely a purchaser of artifacts and services made by, and imported from, others. Unless key components of information and communication technology, artifacts and services are "home-grown," then there is unlikely to be the positive contributions to jobs, education and training that can flow from developments and production stemming from the continuing information revolution. Buying artifacts and services imported from others is the poorest form of "access" – a form that should not lead to complacency or satisfaction.

- *Connectivity, authority, and hierarchy.* There may be relationships among these three concepts that assist in analyzing the factors affecting a country or region. For example, with high connectivity and high degrees of authority in a country, a flattened hierarchy may result. With high connectivity and medium authority, you might have a virtual hierarchy. With high connectivity and low authority, network forms of organization predominate. With low connectivity and high authority, one would expect strict hierarchies. With low connectivity and low authority, one approaches anarchy. In general, the concepts of connectivity and authority create a two-dimensional space within which one might plot points having different forms of hierarchy depending on their position within that space. In very general terms, the Middle East has a strongly hierarchical structure. South Asia primarily has flattened hierarchies. Sub-Saharan Africa is closer to a networking model, with tribes forming the nodes of the network.

- *Altruism.* The policies of OECD (advanced industrialized) nations toward this region should include the concept of altruism, in addition to their standard focus on their own self-interest. The national GDP and yearly individual average income within many countries in the region, compared with those of the rich industrialized nations, is such that the industrialized nations must look beyond "business as usual" in fostering ICT usage and benefits within the region. For an investment that might be trivial for an OECD nation, entire countries might be "wired" to provide country-wide access to wireless communications, or to allow store-and-forward voice messages to be transmitted and received in any village.

- *"NASDAQ Becomes Nirvana."* It was mentioned that in India, in particular, the goal of many of the new ICT entrepreneurs is a listing of their newly-formed company of the NASDAQ stock exchange – a sign of "making it" as well as the potential wealth resulting from an IPO offering. The attraction of such Western images, institutions, and procedures should not be underestimated in the region; in fact, if it is difficult for entrepreneurs in the region to obtain such recognition, they may well contribute to a brain drain from the region of precisely those relatively young, educated, and motivated individuals that could contribute most to regional growth and prosperity.

- *Scalability.* Various of the ICT goods and services might not scale well within the region in question: For example, when a society (e.g., in sub-Saharan Africa) is composed substantially of small villages, it cannot necessarily support the type of information goods and services that larger cities and urban areas can. There are natural and economic limits to ICT diffusion that must be understood.

- *False extrapolation.* There is often a temptation to observe the adoption of various ICT goods and services by a small elite within a country, and extrapolate from that "small n" to the "large N" of the nation's whole population – especially when it is much easier to observe and communicate with the elites within urban or suburban areas. Just because 5% of the population of a country uses cell phones, PCs, the Internet, or whatever, does not mean that the country is at the beginning of "take off" into rapid growth and adoption of that technology. The adoption curve could well taper off at 10%.

Issues to be Addressed

Given the highly diverse and complex nature of the many regions and cultures within the area of the world assigned to this discussion group, we discussed the tensions and issues that any analysis must confront. These include:

- *Technology vs. society as the driver.* In some countries, cultures and regions, one can imagine technology as a driving force: e.g., as new satellite broadcast options become available, they **will** change the information citizens access and what they're informed of. In other countries or cultures, it may well be the case that society (or at least the leadership) retains firm control of information/communication technologies, artifacts and services – perhaps with the concurrence of a majority of citizens – and diffusion of new ICT options remains quite strictly controlled. One analysis or set of conclusions cannot fit all cultures and countries within the region in question.

- *National vs. regional focus.* There are perhaps 20 to 40 countries within the discussion group's purview. For some, the most appropriate analysis is at the country level (e.g., because of strong and distinctive leadership, or distinct policies, within that country). Other groupings of countries (e.g., "Gulf Arab states") might form regions within which some general observations or analyses will hold.

- *Societal structure vs. individual as driver.* In some countries or regions, the institutions and structure of the society will largely determine adoption of ICT. Elsewhere, an individual (e.g., as entrepreneur) can make a substantial difference within an entire country. (Examples in our discussion were cited of persons who had returned to their home country, such as Kenya, and started an Internet Service Provider (ISP) company there that changed the complexion of ICT access within the country.)

- *Enclave economies: isolated or linked.* Within many countries in the region, some enclaves of information/communication technology have grown – some very successfully. (The Bangalore region of India is a strong case in point.) Whether those enclaves affect the entire country or larger region, or remain isolated – perhaps more in contact with Silicon Valley than with neighboring cities – depends strongly on whether individual enclaves within a country become linked with each other, thereby spreading the knowledge, the access, and the opportunities. An analysis of ICT diffusion within a country or region should take this factor into account.

- *Building and testing models.* It would be an interesting exercise to build a heuristic model containing a number of rules regarding the rate, type, and form of ICT developments within a country or region/culture. That model could help predict ICT-related developments given a number of relevant inputs. If such a model were constructed, it might be applied to the period of this present analysis (1999-2003), so that its worth as a predictive model might be assessed by the end of the analysis period.

Change Drivers – The Four Cs

What are the key factors that determine the adoption of, and substantial access to, information and communication technologies within a country or region? Our discussion began with the equation:

$$\text{Structure} + \text{Leadership} \rightarrow \text{ICT Outcome}$$

By that was meant: the two predominant factors leading to a particular ICT outcome are structural factors within a society, plus leadership (normally by a country's leaders, but which could be supplied by individual entrepreneurs and change agents within the country or region). We then grouped the key "change drivers" leading to ICT outcomes into four categories, which can be described by the mnemonically useful rubric: Culture, Competence, Control, Capital.

Culture

Within the category "culture" we include such factors as:

- *Language.* Is the language of the country one of the most world's prominent? If so, many software packages, help manual translations, and so on will be translated into that language, due to the substantial market to be gained. Are many of the country's citizens bilingual? If so, is that second language English (within which so much of ICT and Web information is provided)?

- *Nationalism.* Is the nation or region strongly nationalistic, thereby tending to resist "foreign" influences such as provided by information and communication originating elsewhere?

- *Stratification.* Is the culture of the country or region highly stratified, so that ICT penetration and usage within one stratum is not likely to strongly affect others?

- *Legal framework.* Does the country have a stable, viable legal framework, within which such concepts as intellectual property rights, privacy, and patents can be protected?

- *Vertical authority relationships.* Are the dominant authority relationship vertical (e.g., as in highly hierarchical companies), or does the culture foster small, networked, cooperative arrangements among firms?

- *Trust.* Can business relationships be easily developed outside of tribes, families and other strong social institutions – based on trust relationships? [37]

- *Meritocracy.* Can individuals within the culture succeed based on the merits of their ideas and work, or is success determined by other factors?

- *The concept of information.* What is the concept of information within a society? For example, is it assumed to be a public or private good? If public, then it is difficult to establish property rights to information, which might in turn slow entrepreneurial activities in the ICT sector. If private, then information might be controlled by private-sector organizations in a manner that is monopolistic or otherwise harmful to the society as a whole.

----

[37] For much more discussion of the key role of trust in the development of commerce within societies, see Fukuyama (1995).

Competence

In defining the ICT competence within a society, we included such factors as:

- *Education*. Is education in computer- and communication-related technologies widely available within the country? Is access to such education available based on merit and competence?

- *Training*. Can citizens obtain training in ICT technologies, so that they can provide goods and services needed within the society itself, without needing to rely on outsiders for production, maintenance, and user help facilities?

- *Sophistication of ICT use*. Are citizens of the country mere consumers of the technology and its artifacts and services, or do they produce those goods and services as well?

Capital

Is adequate capital available for the establishment of new ICT-related business ventures within the country? Such capital might include:

- *Internal*. Sources within the country or region itself that provide needed capital for ICT businesses.

- *External*. Is the country or region viewed as a good investment by external parties, so that investment capital can flow into the area? (This of course is at least partly determined by other factors mentioned in this section, such as whether intellectual property rights are honored within a stable system of law.)

- *Physical*. It is important that such infrastructure services as electric power and telecommunications are available, stable, and provided at reasonable cost.

Control

The form of control within a country or region is important in determining the spread of ICT within the area. Factors include:

- *Agency of control*. Is societal control lodged primarily in a government, the military, religious organizations, or the private sector? Differing agencies have different agendas and priorities that in turn affect the area's interest in obtaining and utilizing various information/communication technologies.

- *Form of control.* Is the control that is exercised restrictive and constraining, or promotional and guiding?

—   —   —   —   —

It was noted that, of all the possible country attributes listed above (within our "Four Cs" categories), certain attributes may have differing importance at different stages of ICT development within a country. Figure 11.1 illustrates one possible set of such differences (provided only as an example, until further analysis can be done) at three different parts of the familiar "S" curve of technology adoption.

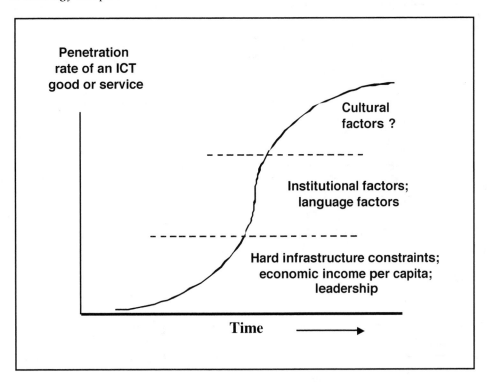

**Figure 11.1 Country Attributes May Have Differing Importance
at Different Stages of Development**

Using the categories developed and defined above, Table 11.1 presents the groups initial, illustrative assessment of these factors for the key countries in the region under consideration.

88

Table 11.1

Assessment of Countries in Africa, Middle East, and South Asia

	Culture	Capital	Competence	Control	Overall
Africa	–	/	/	–	1
S. Africa	/	+	/	/	2.5
Congo	–	–	–	–	0
Mali	–	–	–	–	0
Nigeria	/	/	/	–	1.5
Near East	/	+	/	/	2.5 *
Israel	+	+	+	+	4
Iran	/	+	+	/	3
Syria	/	/	/	–	1.5
S. Arabia	/	+	/	–	2
Iraq	–	/	/	–	1
South Asia	/	/	/	+	2.5
India	+	/	/	+	3
Pakistan	/	–	–	–	0.5
Bangladesh	/	–	/	+	2

The legend for the above table
(used to determine overall scores in the rightmost column):

+ = 1; / = 0.5; – = 0.

This table provides a rough visualization of a possible model. Scorings are approximate at best. The asterisk on the overall score for the Near East is a reminder that the score is skewed by Israel. More likely outcomes for the Islamic Middle east (Arab States plus Iran) is 1,5. For the Arab States alone, it is 1.0.

Technology Issues

The breakout sessions were asked to develop a set of issues or questions to be addressed in the second conference in this series, one more oriented toward ICT trends over the next 10 to 20 years. During our discussion of technology issues, the following basic recommendation emerged: *The technology conference should spent half its time <u>away</u> from high technology, concentrating instead on <u>appropriate</u> technologies for regions such as Africa, Middle East/North Africa, and South Asia.*

This recommendation resulted from our assessment that – for this region in particular – it is vital to consider technologies that are readily absorbable. For example, important technologies over the next decade or two might be those based primarily on radio and wireless, rather than those requiring an elaborate fixed telecommunication infrastructure. Also appropriate would be technologies not requiring much capital, such as software development. A third potentially important factor would be "assistive" artifacts that provide user-computer interfaces not requiring keyboard access or other skills not widespread in the region; technologies such as voice recognition and language translation might allow any regional citizen to approach a kiosk or public access terminal, state a request, and get an answer — possibly an answer that taps onto the increasingly rich resources of the Internet and the World Wide Web, even though that citizen was not fluent in English or one of the other predominant languages on the Web.

However, one of our participants cautioned against generalizations that are too broad, saying: "Don't patronize the region, by concentrating only on cheap technologies. Costs will come down."

Part IV.

Concluding Remarks

12. Major Conference Themes: An Integration and Summary

Conference Rapporteur: Richard Hundley

The conference discussions covered a broad range of topics in considerable depth, and generated a rich set of observations regarding the course of the information revolution throughout the world. A number of major themes emerged during these discussions. We integrate and summarize them here.

A Vision of the Information Revolution Future: "The Great Information Revolution Attractor"

Across the many, highly varied conference discussions, a shared picture emerges of the world towards which the information revolution is driving humanity. This future world should be thought of as a destination towards which all regions and nations are being drawn, at varying rates and from varying distances removed.[38] This "great information revolution attractor" is characterized by a number of interrelated features, including:

- *A rise in "information work" and "information workers,"* as an ever increasing fraction of economic activity and the overall workforce, with a broad range of consequences.

- *New business models,* for the internal organization and functioning of business enterprises, and for their external interactions with customers, suppliers, and competitors.

- *The rise of electronic commerce,* as a major form of economic activity, with accompanying changes in the nature and structure of markets and the elimination of a wide variety of "middlemen" heretofore facilitating economic transitions.

----

[38] One is reminded, by analogy, of the "Great Attractor" in astronomy, a region 200 million light-years away in the direction of the constellation Sagittarius, towards which all of the galaxies in the vicinity of the Milky Way are being drawn. (See Dressler, 1987, and Kraan-Korteweg and Lahav, 1998.)

- *Challenges to the power and authority of the nation state,* for a variety of reasons (including the two immediately following).

- *The creation of a wide variety of sub-national, trans-national and supra-national groupings, communities, organizations and enterprises,* in the business, social, and political realms, often largely beyond the control of individual nation states.

- *An ever increasing porosity of national borders,* to trade and financial flows, to population flows, and to the flow of ideas, entertainment, and culture.

- *Many new winners, and also many new losers.* Some individuals, groups, localities, nations and regions will gain (in power, influence and material well being) as a result of the information revolution; others will lose. All will not share equally in the benefits.

- *New fault lines, within and between nations.* The widening gulfs between the educated, wealthy, and cyber-privileged of all nations, on the one hand, and the not-so-lucky of all nations on the other, will lead to fault lines within nations as well as between nations.

Different regions of the world react differently to this presumed future, to this "great IR attractor": some accept it more or less unquestioningly; some wish to modify it; some strive to achieve it; some try to resist it. We return to these regional differences below.

Some Recurring Concerns Regarding This Future

The conference discussions also reveal a number of widely shared concerns regarding this information revolution future:

Increasing Disparities

As indicated above, this information revolution future (the "great IR attractor") brings with it many winners and many losers, thereby most probably increasing the disparities (economic, social, and political) that exist within societies and between nations. The adverse social and political consequences of these increased disparities are a frequently expressed concern.

These concerns manifest themselves in different forms in different regions of the world.

- In North America, in concerns regarding the disenfranchisement of the "information poor."

- In Europe, in a determination to alleviate such disparities insofar as possible.

- In some regions of the world (e.g., India), in a determination not to be left behind by the information revolution (i.e., to be one of the winners, not one of the losers).

- In other regions of the world (e.g., portions of the Middle East), in a possible reluctance to continuing playing a "losing game" supposedly imposed upon them by the West.[39]

How various nations react to these concerns could well affect the course of the information revolution in their regions.

Impacts on Individual Privacy

The impact of the information revolution on individual privacy is a concern shared widely throughout much (but not all) of the world. This concern stems initially from several factors:

- The strong desire of many individuals, primarily but not exclusively in Western cultures, to retain some control over who knows what about them.

- The transfer of more and more personal information into databases accessible over the Internet.

- The use of this personal information by burgeoning new service businesses, to tailor products to individual tastes, to handle secure electronic transactions, to offer streamlined payment and delivery, and to target advertising and promotion.

There is some ambivalence about this issue, among many of those concerned about the possible loss of privacy, because many people value the personalized products and services that result.

As "ubiquitous" sensor technology spreads throughout the world and increasingly couples physical space to cyberspace,[40] these privacy concerns are broadened to include possible "sinister" uses of such surveillance technology (by governments, etc.).

These privacy concerns are strongest today in Europe and North America, but present elsewhere as well. How various nations react to these concerns could

----

[39] What such nations could do to get out of this "losing game" remains to be seen.

[40] See p. 9 for examples of such ubiquitous sensors.

also affect the course of the information revolution in different regions of the world.

Impact on National Cultures

The increasing porosity of national borders to the flow of ideas, entertainment, and culture has facilitated the spread of Western, and particularly U.S., culture throughout the world. Many people feel that the continued vitality and possibly even long-term existence of their national cultures may be threatened by this process. These concerns manifest themselves in many non-Western settings (e.g., throughout much of the Islamic world), and also in some Western settings (e.g., France, Canada, etc.)

These concerns are widespread but by no means universal. How various nations react to these concerns could also affect the course of the information revolution in their regions.

Governance in the Information Age

The information age changes both the character and distribution of political power, as well as reconfiguring the processes of governance.

Regarding the distribution of political power: The power of the state is being modified as new non-state actors are being empowered, including transnational business organizations, sub- and transnational special affinity groups (ranging across the religious, ethnic, professional, criminal, etc., spectra), and other non-governmental organizations (NGOs).

This leads to various concerns: What will the role and authority of national governments be vis-a-vis these emerging non-state actors. Will there be new allocations of power? Will power be shared in new and different ways? Who will be accountable in the future information age? Will more and more decisions affecting nation states be made by actors not accountable to the citizens of those states.

Such concerns are just beginning to manifest themselves.[41] How they play out could also affect the course of the information revolution.

----

[41] The demonstrations at the World Trade Organization meeting in Seattle in early December 1999 (after this conference was over) may be an early manifestation of such concerns.

Regarding the process of governance: Traditional mechanisms are becoming increasingly problematic, as the information revolution allows action beyond the reach of national governments. For example:

- E-commerce will make transaction taxes (e.g., sales taxes) more difficult to collect. This could lead to more reliance on other types of taxes.

- Regulation and licensing will become increasingly difficult when service providers are beyond national jurisdictions.

- Limits on offensive or dangerous information (.e.g., pornography, hate literature, bomb-making instructions) will not always be honored by others.

In these and other areas, governments will have to find new mechanisms of governance, or will have to create new, near-universal international control regimes.

Inability of Nations/Societies to Go Their Own Ways

Economies of scale in information-rich activities are potentially very large. For this reason, nations/societies will pay an increasing price for being different. For example:

- It will be hard for western Europe and the United States to maintain different standards for data privacy and protection.

- Widely disseminated content -- video, text, etc. -- will have a big cost advantage over content tailored to a specific small market. For this reason, nations such as Canada will find it difficult to maintain "Canadian content."

- A handful of technical standards (regarding information and communication formats, etc.) will likely dominate throughout the world, even if these are less than ideal in certain settings.

Because nations/societies will be less able to tailor information services to their specific needs, we must expect frictions over the character of the emerging global services.

Some Key Uncertainties Regarding the Future

All is not clear regarding this information revolution future. Key uncertainties include:

The Future Course of IT Penetration

How deeply and quickly will the Internet and the accompanying information revolution penetrate, in various regions of the world? How many of the information-poor will it reach in the advanced nations? How fully will it reach into the less developed nations?

How IT penetration plays out will affect the balance of winners and losers in the new information age, both within nations and between nations.

Uncertainties Regarding "Proximity" in the Information Age

In principle, information technology can be used to replace physical proximity with functional proximity, for many human activities. In practice, however, face-to-face interactions still seem to be needed in many circumstances.

This leads to a number of questions: What constitutes effective "proximity" in the information age? When are face-to-face interactions still needed? When will interactions via cyberspace suffice?

In addressing these questions, some find it useful to draw a distinction between "explicit knowledge" and "tacit knowledge."[42] In this view, physical proximity is not required for the exchange of explicit knowledge; it is required, however, for the effective sharing of tacit knowledge.

How this question plays out will affect the geographic dispersion or clustering of many different types of economic activity, as the information age progresses. Will various activities be dispersed widely (e.g., through out-sourcing or "off-shoring"), or concentrated in geographical clusters?

---

[42] Roughly speaking, in this context explicit knowledge is knowledge that is clear cut, unambiguous, and well understood by all. Tacit knowledge is knowledge that is implied or inferred, and is not generally understood by all. Explicit knowledge is generally available. Tacit knowledge rests in the minds and creative behaviors of individuals and teams, both within and between organizations. See Porter (1998).

The Future Evolution of "The Great IR Attractor"

The future world described by "the great information revolution attractor" is not a static world, with characteristics fixed forever in time. Rather, it changes as new technology developments occur. It is a "moving target" towards which the world is being drawn.

This leads to several related questions: How will the current technology drivers of the information revolution evolve over the next 10–20 years? What new technology drivers may emerge during that period of time? What new characteristics might "the great IR attractor" assume over the next 10–20 years?

These questions will be the subject of a future conference.

Differences in Regional Emphasis Regarding The Future

There are differing emphases in various regions around the world, insofar as the information revolution future is concerned. As reflected in the breakout group discussions during the conference, these differing emphases appear to be as follows:

North America

The predominant North American attitude could be characterized as "information revolution determinism." The information revolution is viewed as being inevitable. It will run its course no matter what. Backlashes of various forms are expected to occur, but these are not considered likely to sufficiently retard or modify the process.

Concerns are expressed regarding the disenfranchisement of the "information poor," leading to increased social stress and stratification. Conflicts over privacy are also expected.

But in the end, the information revolution is expected to prevail. North America is in the camp that accepts the information revolution as being more or less irresistible and socially beneficial.

Europe

In Europe there is much more of a focus on realizing (economic) value from the information revolution <u>while</u> at the same time maintaining and protecting existing cultural and social values. Europeans believe that they can and must actively shape the course of the information revolution to achieve these ends.

There is much more of a determination to alleviate disparities (between winners and losers) insofar as possible, than appears to be the case in the U.S.[43] There are also major concerns about maintaining privacy.[44]

Europe is in the camp that wants to shape the course of the information revolution, to suit its own ends. To what extent it can do this remains to be seen.

Asia Pacific Region

The emphasis in the Asia Pacific region is on realizing value from the information revolution -- primarily economic value. There is less concern with disparities, and less concern about privacy (possibly because of the "communal" nature of Asian culture). The prevailing attitude appears to be: "Don't worry about losers; concentrate on becoming a winner." There appears to be widespread confidence that many/most Asian countries can become winners.

The Asia Pacific region appears to be in the camp that is striving to achieve the information revolution, striving to reach "the great IR attractor," and is generally confident that it can do so.

Middle East, Africa, and South Asia

This part of the world is often characterized by strong differences in focus between leadership/elite groups and mass citizenry. Many leaders/elites want, and use, the benefits of information technology -- but are wary of its influences on the citizenry.

In some major nations (e.g., India), there is a determination not to be left behind by the information revolution (i.e., to be one of the winners, not one of the losers). As one conference participant from this part of the world said: "We missed out on the industrial revolution; we don't want to miss out on the information revolution." In these nations, there is much discussion of what it takes to get access to and successfully exploit information technology, to raise the nation/region (economically, socially, etc.) But it often proves difficult to expand

----

[43] Canada may be closer to Europe than to the U.S. on this issue.

[44] Currently, these concerns regarding privacy are greater in Europe than in the U.S.

"islands" of information-revolution expertise, both within nations and to the rest of the countries in the region.

Some other nations' leaders/elites in the region may already anticipate losing, and may be starting to imagine dire consequences. But many citizens are unaffected and unconcerned now, and will be into the indefinite future.

Especially in this region, much of the information revolution emphasis may be on non-Internet technologies: e.g., wireless telephony, accessible satellite TV broadcasts, photo copier and fax machines, audio and video cassettes, etc.

Many in the Middle East, Africa, and South Asia want to use the information revolution to better themselves and their countries, but with widely varying abilities to do so.

Some Interesting Analytic Constructs

A number of interesting analytic constructs were proposed during the conference, including:

The Technology, Artifact, Roles/Usage Model

This model, illustrated schematically in Figure 12.1, is being developed by Crosby (2000) to describe the development and application of technology in various cultures. In this model: "technology" denotes an organized body of knowledge (e.g., information technology); "artifact" denotes the products of a technology (e.g., the desktop computer); "roles and usage" denotes applications of an artifact (e.g., desktop publishing).

This model was used by the Asia Pacific breakout group in discussing the course of the information revolution in its region. We intend applying it more broadly during our future efforts to chart the worldwide course of the information revolution.

102

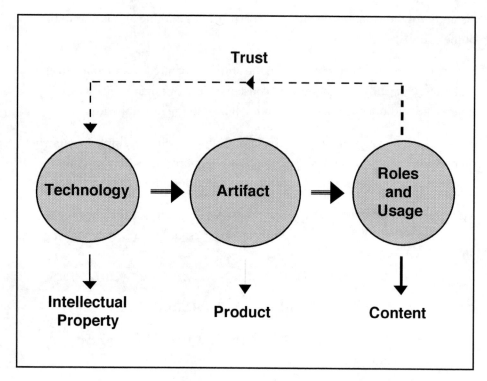

Figure 12.1 The Technology, Artifact, Roles/Usage Model

The Four C's

The Middle East, Africa, and South Asia breakout group identified four factors that, acting as drivers or impediments of change, determine the adoption of, and substantial access to, information and communication technologies (ICT):[45]

- *Culture,* which includes as sub-factors language, nationalism, stratification, legal framework, vertical authority relationships, trust, meritocracy, and the concept of information (within the society).

- *Competence,* which includes as sub-factors education, training, and the sophistication of ICT use.

- *Capital,* which includes as sub-factors internal capital sources, external capital sources, and physical infrastructures (e.g., electric power, telecommunications).

- *Control,* which includes as sub-factors agency of control and form of control.

----

[45] More details of this model are given in Section 11.

The Middle East, Africa, and South Asia breakout group used this model to assess the capabilities of key countries in their region to access, adopt, and exploit information and communication technologies. We intend applying it more broadly during our future efforts to chart the worldwide course of the information revolution.

Driving Factors and Stunting Factors

The Asia Pacific breakout group used a set of "driving" and "stunting" factors, shown in Table 12.1, to characterize the capability of the region as a whole and of individual nations across the technology–artifacts–roles/usage space: i.e., the capability to develop new information technology or new IR artifacts, or to use technology and artifacts developed by others.

Table 12.1

Driving and Stunting Factors

	Technology (Intellectual Property)	Artifact (Product)	Usage (Content)
Driving Factors	• Education • Equity capital access • Venture spirit • Local market potential	• Tax policy • Plentiful, low-cost labor • "ISP" effect	• Consumer wealth • Taxation policy • "ISP" effect • Quality and availability of service
Stunting Factors	• Over regulation • Government policy • Intellectual property right violations • Monopolies	• Low mfg./process technology • Distribution and sourcing • Legacy systems	• Censorship • Lack of credit • Trust of product • Language

The driving and stunting factors identified by the Asia Pacific group appear to be a subset of the "Four Cs" enumerated by the Middle East, Africa, and South Asia group. Our intent is to combine these constructs during our future efforts, using the "Four Cs"(or an expanded set thereof) as an assessment device across the technology–artifacts–roles/usage space.

Some Inferred Candidate National Models of the Information Revolution Future

The conference discussions did not explicitly develop a comprehensive set of models of what the information revolution future might be like in various nations and regions throughout the world. However, from those discussions it is possible to infer the following candidate set of national models of the information revolution future:

- *IR Achievers.* These are nations that have substantially attained most/all of the characteristics of "the great IR attractor." Information work and information workers represent an ever increasing fraction of the economy and the workforce; new, information-based business models and electronic commerce are spreading throughout the business and financial communities; many/most segments of society are well into the information age, and substantially "wired" into the global arena. Australia is one example (among several) of a nation that is today an IR Achiever.[46]

- *IR Drivers.* These are nations that go well beyond being merely an IR Achiever. They not only have attained most/all of the (then) existing characteristics of "the great IR attractor," but go well beyond this to create new characteristics, new manifestations of the information revolution. The U.S. is the best, but not the only, example of an IR Driver nation today.

- *IR Strivers.* These are nations that are working very hard to reach" the great IR attractor," but still have a considerable way to go, with the final result still in some doubt. Taiwan is an example of a nation that today is an IR Striver.

- *IR Modifiers.* These are nations that are not satisfied with one or more characteristics of "the great IR attractor" towards which they are being drawn, and wish to actively shape and modify those characteristics to suit their own ends. They are trying to change the course of the information revolution, insofar as it applies to them. Singapore is a clear example today of an IR Modifier. It is trying to realize all of the benefits of the information

---

[46] This country assignment, as well as the others that follow, is very preliminary and meant merely to be illustrative.

revolution in the economic sphere, while at the same time strictly controlling developments in the social/cultural sphere.[47]

- *IR Veneer Societies.* These are nations in which a small fraction of the society is participating in the information revolution and well into the information age, with the vast bulk of the population still in the industrial or even the agricultural age. India is a clear example today of an IR Veneer Society. It has geographical clusters of high technology (e.g., around Bangalore), with software (and other) companies fully participating in the global information economy and some even on the NASDAQ stock exchange. At the same time, the vast majority of Indian citizens (probably 95% or more) are uninvolved in and unaffected by the information revolution.

- *IR Left-Behinds.* These are nations that have been more or less totally left behind by the information revolution. It has passed them by, for whatever reasons (most often socioeconomic). They are not involved, and largely unaware. Zaire is once such example, today, of an IR Left-Behind.

- *IR Luddites.* These are nations that, for whatever reason, actively oppose the course of the information revolution. They want to opt out. They don't want to participate. They don't want it happening in their society. They are more or less totally opposed to the changes being brought on by the information revolution. North Korea may be an example today of an IR Luddite.

- *Sore IR Losers.* These are nations that are unhappy left-behinds. They feel themselves losing out, as the information revolution progresses, and they are not happy with this outcome. It is not clear that any nation fits into this category today. But some could in the future.

This set of future models appears to span the range of situations suggested during the conference discussions. Most nations and regions should fit into one or another of these categories, insofar as the information revolution is concerned.[48] We intend using this set of models a point of departure during our future efforts to chart the worldwide course of the information revolution.[49]

In addition to this set of models, the European breakout group developed a set of four more specialized models -- *atomisation, corporatisation, regionalisation, and dynamic conservatism* – to describe that nature of the societal interactions in an information-revolution society. These models are described in Section 8.

----

[47] Many doubt that Singapore can achieve its aims in this regard. Whether it ultimately succeeds or fails is immaterial to its present-day designation as an IR Modifier.

[48] At any given time, some of these models could be empty sets, and some nations could be in more than one category.

[49] During these future efforts, this set of models will most likely evolve and change.

13. What Comes Next

Conference Rapporteur: Richard Hundley

As indicated earlier, this conference was merely the beginning of a multi-year effort to chart the future worldwide course of the information revolution. We feel that this conference was a good first step, in which we accomplished the following:

- We developed a shared vision of the information revolution future towards which the world is being drawn.

- We identified:

    - Some recurring concerns regarding this future.

    - Some key uncertainties regarding this future.

    - Apparent differences in regional emphasis regarding this future.

    - Some interesting analytic constructs.

- We laid the groundwork from which to develop models of possible alternative information-revolution futures in different countries.

- We began assembling an intellectual team to address this problem.

What comes next are some questions for the technologists, a number of topics requiring further work, and after that, additional conferences. We discuss each of these briefly in turn.

Questions for the Technologists

The November 1999 conference has posed two categories of questions for the information technologists:

108

A. How may technology, artifact, and roles/usage developments[50] over the next 10-20 years add to the characteristics of "the great IR attractor"? Such developments could include:

- Technology, artifact, and roles/usage developments leading to new business paradigms -- beyond the current e-commerce paradigm.

- Technology, artifact, and roles/usage developments leading to new paradigms in education,[51] medicine and health care, entertainment, or other societal areas.

- Technology, artifact, and roles/usage developments that increasingly couple cyberspace to physical space.

- Technology, artifact, and roles/usage developments leading to new computing paradigms (e.g., quantum computing, DNA-based computing, etc.) -- during the next 20 years.[52]

B. How may technology developments over the next 10-20 years facilitate the access of have-nots to the information revolution, or otherwise cause differential impacts in various regions of the world? Such developments could include:

- Developments that avoid (or overcome) requirements for education (e.g., the current keyboard-style interface) and/or cultural change in order to effectively access information technology.

- Developments that reduce the amount of infrastructure (e.g., electric power grid, telecommunications network, etc.) required to effectively access information technology.

- Developments that remove (or overcome) language barriers.

- Developments that could enable some nations or regions in the developing world to skip stages that the developed world has gone through in the past (e.g., skipping land-lines and going right to a wireless-based telecommunications network).

These questions will be addressed during a Spring 2000 conference.

----

[50] We are using the terminology "technology, artifact, and roles/usage" here in the sense described in Section 10.

[51] Particularly entertainment viewed as a venue through which social, political, and cultural values are transferred from one nation or society to another.

[52] The 1997 ACM conference (see Denning and Metcalfe, 1997, and Denning, 1999) identified a number of new computing paradigms that could come to fruition over the next 50 years. The time horizon for our current effort is only 20 years. So the question is: which of these new computing paradigms are likely to come to fruition during this shorter time period?

Topics Requiring More Work

The November 1999 conference identified a number of topics requiring further work. These include:

- *Models of the information revolution.* We need to flesh out the set of models presented in Section 12 in much more detail, and begin "assigning" nations to each of the various models.

- *The information revolution in Latin America.* We need a small workshop focused on this subject, to broaden and deepen our understanding of the course of the information revolution in this part of the world.

- *The future course of IT penetration.* Papers presented at the November conference presented a quantitative picture of the state of IT penetration throughout the world today, focusing primarily on the Internet. We need to expand this picture beyond the Internet, to other aspects of IT technology, and develop quantitative projections of future IT penetration throughout the world, insofar as possible.

- *"Proximity" in the information age.* We need to better understand which societal activities will cluster geographically, and which will disperse.

These topics will be worked on during the coming months.

And After That: Additional Conferences

Once the above items are (substantially) complete, we anticipate holding two more major international conferences, preferably in Europe and in Asia, to expose and vet our results before a wider international audience, thereby broadening and deepening our models of the future course of the information revolution throughout the world.

Appendix

A. Conference Participants

Dr. Jon B. Alterman (UNITED STATES)
> Middle East Program Officer, United States Institute of Peace

Professor Kim V. Andersen (DENMARK)
> Department of Informatics, Copenhagen Business School

Dr. Robert H. Anderson (UNITED STATES)
> Senior Information Scientist and Head, Information Sciences Group, RAND

Professor Vallampadugai S. Arunachalam (INDIA)
> Engineering & Public Policy Department and Robotics Institute, Carnegie Mellon University

Dr. Tora Kay Bikson (UNITED STATES)
> Senior Behavioral Scientist, RAND

Mr. Taylor Boas (UNITED STATES)
> Carnegie Endowment for International Peace

Professor Paul Bracken (UNITED STATES)
> School of Management, Yale University

Mr. Clinton C. Brooks (UNITED STATES)
> Corporate Knowledge Strategist, National Security Agency

Professor Eric Brousseau (FRANCE)
> Centre ATOM, Universite de Paris I Pantheon Sorbonne

Professor William Caelli (AUSTRALIA)
> School of Data Communications, Queensland University of Technology

Mr. Colin Crook (UNITED STATES)
> Senior Fellow, Wharton School; Former Senior Technology Officer, Citibank

Dr. James Dewar (UNITED STATES)
> Senior Mathematician, RAND

Dr. William Drake (UNITED STATES)
   Senior Associate, and Director of the Project on the Information
   Revolution and World Politics, Carnegie Endowment for International
   Peace

Professor Francis Fukuyama (UNITED STATES)
   Institute Of Public Policy, George Mason University

Dr. Lawrence K. Gershwin (UNITED STATES)
   National Intelligence Officer for Science & Technology,
   National Intelligence Council

Mr. David C. Gompert (UNITED STATES)
   Vice President, National Security Research Division and
   Director, National Defense Research Institute, RAND

Professor Sy Goodman (UNITED STATES)
   University of Arizona, Georgia Tech, and Stanford University

Dr. David Gordon (UNITED STATES)
   National Intelligence Officer for Economics and Global Issues,
   National Intelligence Council

Dr. Jerrold Green (UNITED STATES)
   Senior Political Scientist, Director of International Development,
   and Director, Center for Middle East Public Policy, RAND

Dr. Eugene C. Gritton (UNITED STATES)
   Director, Acquisition and Technology Policy Program, RAND

Dr. Richard O. Hundley (UNITED STATES)
   Senior Physical Scientist, RAND

Dr. Paul Kozemchak (UNITED STATES)
   Special Assistant to the Director, Defense Advanced Research Projects
   Agency

Dr. John Kriese (UNITED STATES)
   Chief Scientist, Defense Intelligence Agency

Ms. Ellen Laipson (UNITED STATES)
   Vice Chairman, National Intelligence Council

Dr. Martin Libicki (UNITED STATES)
   Senior Policy Analyst, RAND

Mr. John Mabberley (BRITAIN)
      Managing Director, DERAtec, Defence Evaluation and Research Agency

Ms. Yuko Maeda (JAPAN)
      Nomura Research Institute America

Professor Mark Mason (UNITED STATES)
      School of Foreign Service, Georgetown University

Mr. Hideo Miyashita (JAPAN)
      General Manager, Center for Cyber Communities Initiative,
      Nomura Research Institute Ltd.

Dr. James Mulvenon (UNITED STATES)
      Associate Political Scientist, RAND

Dr. C. Richard Neu (UNITED STATES)
      Senior Economist and Associate Director, Project Air Force, RAND

Mr. Yoshiyuki Noguchi (JAPAN)
      President, Nomura Research Institute America

Dr. William Nolte (UNITED STATES)
      Director, Outreach and Strategic Planning, National Intelligence Council

Professor M. J. Norton (BRITAIN)
      Head of Electronic Business, Institute of Directors

Mr. Ian Pearson (BRITAIN)
      BT's Futurologist, British Telecommunications

Professor Larry Press (UNITED STATES)
      Chairman, CIS Department, California State University at Dominguez
      Hills

Ms. Betsy Quint-Moran (UNITED STATES)
      Strategic Assessments Group, Office of Transnational Issues,
      Central Intelligence Agency

Dr. Enid Schoettle (UNITED STATES)
      Special Advisor to the Chairman, National Intelligence Council

Dr. Brian Shaw (UNITED STATES)
      Deputy National Intelligence Officer for Science & Technology,
      National Intelligence Council

114

Professor Ernest Wilson (UNITED STATES)
        Director, Center for International Development and Conflict
        Management, University of Maryland at College Park

Mr. Robert Worden (UNITED STATES)
        Federal Research Division, Library of Congress

Ms. Lily Wu (UNITED STATES)
        Former Director, Equity Research, Salomon Smith Barney, Hong Kong
        and San Francisco, currently Acting CFO, Disappearing Inc. and
        MovieQ.com

Mr. Boris Zhikharevich (RUSSIA)
        Head, Strategic Planning Department, Leontief Centre, St. Petersburg

B. Conference Agenda

Tuesday, November 16

Opening Plenary Session

Moderator: Richard Hundley (RAND)

8:30 am	Welcome to RAND	David Gompert (RAND)
8:45 am	Welcome by the National Intelligence Council	Lawrence Gershwin (NIC)
9:00 am	Conference Introduction	Richard Hundley (RAND)
9:30 am	Social and Organizational Consequences of the Transition into the Information Age	Francis Fukuyama (George Mason University)
10:00 am	Audience Discussion	
10:30 am	Break	
11:00 am	Information Technology Trends – The Next 20 Years	Robert Anderson (RAND)
11:30 am	Worldwide Information Revolution Demographics	Larry Press (Cal State Dominguez Hills)
12:00 noon	Audience Discussion	
12:30 pm	Session Ends	

Tuesday, November 16 (continued)

The Political/Governmental Dimension
of the Information Revolution

Moderator: David Gompert (RAND)

1:30 pm	The Information Revolution, National Sovereignty, and Political Change	William Drake (Carnegie Endowment for International Peace)
2:00 pm	The Role of Nationalism in the Information Revolution	Paul Bracken (Yale University)
2:30 pm	Audience Discussion	
3:15 pm	Session Ends	

The Business/Financial Dimension
of the Information Revolution

Moderator: C. Richard Neu (RAND)

3:45 pm	E-Commerce - Clusters in a Global Economy?	Jim Norton (Institute of Directors)
4:15 pm	New Business Models Driven by the Information Revolution	Colin Crook (Wharton School)
4:45 pm	Audience Discussion	
5:30 pm	Session Ends	

Wednesday, November 17

The Social/Cultural Dimension of the Information Revolution

Moderator: Tora Bikson (RAND)

8:30 am	The Lexus Hits an Olive Tree: the social and cultural impact of the information revolution in the developing world	Jon Alterman (United States Institute of Peace)
9:00 am	Audience Discussion	
9:45 am	Session Ends	

Modifying Factors: How the Information Revolution May Proceed Differently in Various Regions of the World

Moderator: Jerrold Green (RAND)

10:15 am	The Present Status and Characteristics of the Cyber Revolution in Japan	Hideo Miyashita (Nomura Research Institute)
10:45 am	Bridging the Digital Divide: The Indian Story	V. S. Arunachalam (Carnegie Mellon University)
11:15 am	The Information Revolution at the Margins: E-Economy, E-Security and E-Equity in Africa	Ernest Wilson (University of Maryland)
11:45 am	Audience Discussion	
12:15 pm	Introduction to the Breakout Groups	Richard Hundley (RAND)
12:30 pm	Session Ends	

118

Wednesday, November 17 (continued)

Breakout Group Sessions

1:30 pm Separate Breakout Group sessions discussing modifying factors and possible futures in various regions of the world

North, Central, and South America

Discussion Leader: C. Richard Neu (RAND)
Rapporteur: Martin Libicki (RAND)

Europe

Discussion Leader: Ian Pearson (British Telecommunications)
Rapporteur: Tora Bikson (RAND)

Middle East, Africa, and South Asia

Discussion Leader: Ernest Wilson (Univ. of Maryland)
Rapporteur: Robert Anderson (RAND)

Asia Pacific

Discussion Leader: James Mulvenon (RAND)
Rapporteur: James Dewar (RAND)

5:00 pm Breakout sessions end

7:30 pm

Conference Banquet

After Dinner Speaker

James Dewar (RAND)

*The Information Age and the Printing Press:
Looking Backward to See Ahead*

Thursday, November 18

Breakout Group Sessions (continued)

8:30 am   Breakout Group sessions resume (for second thoughts and closure)

10:00 an   Breakout sessions end

Closing Plenary Session
Moderator: Richard Hundley (RAND)

10:30 am   Breakout Group Reports   Breakout Group leaders, rapporteurs and participants

Breakout Groups report back to entire conference on the course and result of their discussions

12:30 pm   Closing comments   Richard Hundley (RAND)

Lawrence Gershwin (NIC)

1:00 pm   Conference adjourns

Bibliography

(Cabinet Office, 1999) *e-commerce@its.best.uk,* Performance and Innovation Unit, Cabinet Office, London, September 1999.

(Crosby, 2000) Eleanor Crosby, *Classifying Technologies: A New Approach to Classification in Archaeology,* to be published.

(Denning and Metcalfe, 1997) Peter J. Denning and Robert M. Metcalfe, editors, *Beyond Calculation: The Next Fifty Years of Computing,* Springer-Verlag, New York, 1997.

(Denning, 1999) Peter J. Denning, editor, *Talking Back to the Machine: Computers and Human Aspiration,* Copernicus, Springer-Verlag, New York, 1999.

(Dressler, 1987) Alan Dressler, "The Large-Scale Streaming of Galaxies," *Scientific American,* September 1987.

(Fukuyama, 1995) Francis Fukuyama, *Trust: The Social Virtues and the Creation of Prosperity,* Free Press Paperbacks, Simon & Schuster, 1995.

(Kraan-Korteweg and Lahav, 1998) Renee C. Kraan-Korteweg and Ofer Lahav, "Galaxies behind the Milky Way," *Scientific American,* October 1999, pp. 50-57.

(Nelson, 1993) Richard R. Nelson, *National Innovation Systems: A Comparative Analysis,* Oxford University Press, New York, 1993.

(Porter, 1998) Michael E. Porter, "Clusters and the New Economics of Competition," *Harvard Business Review,* 1998, pp. 77-90.